The NEW What Can You Do with a Law Degree?

A Lawyer's Guide to Career Satisfaction Inside, Outside & Around the Law

LARRY RICHARD, Ph.D.
TANYA HANSON, J.D.

DecisionBooks
SEATTLE, WASHINGTON

Published by LawyerAvenue Press and its imprint DecisionBooks

Cover design by Elizabeth Watson
Interior design by Rose Michelle Taverniti
Founding author Deborah Arron

Volume discounts available from LawyerAvenue Press. Email to editor@ LawyerAvenue.com, or write to Avenue Productions, 4701 SW Admiral Way #278, Seattle WA 98116.

Library of Congress CIP Data

Richard, Larry, J. D.
  The new what can you do with a law degree : a lawyer's guide to career satisfaction inside, outside & around the law / Larry Richard & Tanya Hanson.—[New ed.].
      p. cm.
  Rev. ed. of: What can you do with a law degree : a lawyer's guide to career alternatives inside, outside & around the law / Deborah Arron. 5th ed. 2004.
  ISBN 978-0-940675-71-1 (alk. paper)
  1. Law—Vocational guidance—United States. 2. Lawyers—United States. I. Hanson, Tanya. II. Arron, Deborah L., 1950- What can you do with a law degree. III. Title.
  KF297.A875 2012
  340.23'73--dc23
                      2012024605

THIS BOOK IS DEDICATED TO THE MEMORY OF MY PARENTS,
MAE AND HOWARD RICHARD—
MY FIRST SOURCE OF CAREER INSPIRATION. —LR

THIS BOOK IS DEDICATED TO MY PARENTS
FOR THEIR UNWAVERING BELIEF IN ME. —TH

CONTENTS

Acknowledgements

About the Authors

Introduction

Section One: You Are Here   *1*

Chapter 1   What's Your Career Identity?   *2*

Chapter 2   Why This Book Was Written (and for Whom)   *4*

Chapter 3   The Nature of Transition   *9*

Section Two: Who Are You?   *13*

Chapter 4   The Case for Self-Assessment   *14*

Chapter 5   Introducing The Lawyer Career Satisfaction Model℠   *17*

Chapter 6   Does Your Job Fit Your Values?   *31*

Chapter 7   Does Your Job Fit Your Psychological Needs?   *49*

Chapter 8   Does Your Job Fit Your Communication Style?   *57*

Chapter 9   Does Your Job Fit Your Motivated Skills?   *69*

Chapter 10   Does Your Job Fit Your Career Interests?   *80*

Section Three: Where Are You Going?   *89*

Chapter 11   Identifying Your Ideal Job   *90*

Chapter 12   The Case for Solo Practice   *103*

Chapter 13   Finding Work Inside, Outside & Around the Law   *111*

Chapter 14   Putting Your Best Foot Forward   *124*

Chapter 15   The Personal Obstacles to Career Satisfaction   *134*

Chapter 16   Should I Leave the Law?   *143*

Chapter 17   The Disengagement Process   *146*

Chapter 18   Your Support Network   *160*

Appendices   *163*

A   800+ Ways to Use Your Law Degree   *164*

B   Legal & Law-Related Certificate & Credential-Building Programs   *174*

C   Getting the Most from Career & Outplacement Counseling   *195*

D   Homework Assignments   *202*

E   The Values Card Sort Exercise   *206*

ACKNOWLEDGEMENTS

Writing a book is not a one-person job. I could not have written this book without my co-author, Tanya Hanson. Her insights, wisdom, persistence, writing and editing skills, and thoughtful collaboration have been more helpful than words can convey. I also owe a debt of gratitude to the hundreds of lawyers that I had the privilege of coaching over the years. I learned so much from them as we worked together to explore their career paths forward. I am equally indebted to the numerous other career counselors, psychologists, guidance counselors, professors and other vocational professionals who have given me ideas, critiqued my theories, and generally supported me as I developed this model. Our fine editor, Mark Jaroslaw, deserves the lion's share of credit for this book for his vision, persistence, steady hand, and creativity in shaping the direction of this entire project. Indispensable as all these others have been, this book simply wouldn't have been written without the support and encouragement of my wife/friend/editor/traveling companion/love of my life D'Arcy, whose deep insight, eye for detail, perceptiveness about people and moral support were all incalculable aids in my writing of this book.—LR

I am extraordinarily grateful for all the support I have received throughout this endeavor. I would like to acknowledge a few individuals for their special contribution to this work. To all those who reviewed versions of the manuscript, thank you for shaping what it would become. To my law school friends and colleagues, thank you for your stories and for providing inspiration for the work. To my first mentor, Karen Saul, thank you for supporting my desire to take the path less traveled. To my friends, old and new, thank you for convincing me that this book was a good idea, encouraging me to keep going, and celebrating with me when it was finished. To my parents, thank you for never doubting that this book would be written. To my life coach, Wendy Hupperich, thank you for helping me find my voice. To my coauthor, Larry Richard, thank you for your partnership and for generously sharing your brilliant work. I have learned so much from you. —TH

ABOUT THE AUTHORS

Dr. *Larry Richard* is recognized as the leading expert on the lawyer personality. Since 1981, he has counseled over 500 lawyers and has gathered personality data from over 40,000 lawyers. He holds a J.D. from the University of Pennsylvania, and Ph.D. in Psychology from Temple University. He spent the first 15 years of his practice counseling lawyers on career change and career planning. Formerly a consultant with Hildebrandt, he now heads his own firm, LawyerBrain LLC, which helps law firms with leadership and change management issues.

Tanya *Hanson, JD*, is a career coach who works with lawyers and other professionals to discover their unique career identity and find satisfying work. Ms. Hanson is also an attorney with the Oregon State Bar Professional Liability Fund, where she edits publications and helps coordinate seminars that assist lawyers in their personal and professional lives. After leaving private practice, she worked in financial publishing and taught in a paralegal program. Ms. Hanson has spoken about her career transition at the Lawyers in Transition program facilitated by the Oregon Attorney Assistance Program.

INTRODUCTION

Identity is the deepest, most stable part of our personalities, and thus changes little over time.

The more we base our career choices on how well they fit with our identity, the more assured we can be that the choices will remain satisfying over the long term. *The New What Can You Do With a Law Degree* introduces a model for career satisfaction based on the well-established principle that the better the fit between a person's career identity and his or her job, the greater the person's long-term career satisfaction. The model applies both to lawyers who want to find satisfaction in the traditional practice of law, and to those of you seeking satisfaction through alternative work arrangements or career choices.

To help you find your own unique identity, this book will start by discussing the need for an inner-directed approach to career satisfaction, and will explain why lawyers tend to approach the career change process backwards. I will then introduce the key elements of **The Lawyer Career Satisfaction Model**ˢᴹ, devoting an entire chapter to each element. Then I will explain how all of this fits together, and how you can discover your own satisfying career criteria. Finally, I will give you some advice about making a transition, and finding resources to assist you in the job search and change process.

Each chapter has assignments for you to complete as you work through the chapter. Yes, you can skip them, and still get valuable insights from this book. But the most valuable insights are going to come from you. So, I strongly encourage you to spend some time reflecting on the questions and giving thoughtful answers. I compiled these exercises during my years as a career counselor to lawyers. They have helped many other lawyers in their self-discovery process, and they can help you, too.

This book is no different from many endeavors in life: you get out of it what you put into it.

If you invest time and energy into the process of self-assessment, you will be rewarded with greater self-knowledge. In turn, this will allow you to make more informed, enlightened decisions regarding your career, instead of throwing darts at the board. No one can make this most personal decision for you, but we can shed some light on your path and guide you through the process of self-exploration.

As former practicing lawyers, both Tanya and I have gone through this process of transition ourselves, and we know what it feels like to find yourself at a professional crossroads: confused and unsure of how to proceed. We also know how satisfying it can be to get past that, and transition to a satisfying career. We invite you to take the journey with us.

—LARRY RICHARD, JD/PH.D., TANYA HANSON, JD
AUGUST, 2012

SECTION ONE
YOU ARE HERE

Chapter 1   What's Your Career Identity?   *2*

Chapter 2   Why This Book Was Written (and for Whom)   *4*

Chapter 3   The Nature of Transition   *9*

CHAPTER 1

What's Your Career Identity?

If you're like most lawyers facing a career transition, your first thought is, *"What's out there?"* That is, what jobs or opportunities are available that I could do with my legal background? A much more successful strategy for making a satisfying career transition is to ask, *"What's in here?"* That is, what is my career identity? Because common sense—now backed up by research—tells us that the better the fit between a person and his or her job, *the more satisfied the person will be.*

Being a lawyer is not just a job, it's an identity.

It defines who we are, how we think, and what we believe we can do in the world. And the process of becoming a lawyer is much more than job training. It involves the instilling of values, ideals, and a special type of thinking, and it has its rituals, codes of behavior, and initiation rites. Career dissatisfaction, therefore, can be demoralizing because it undercuts our very *identity*. It can't be dismissed as just a failure of the 9-to-5 portion of our lives. And for this reason career satisfaction is especially important for lawyers and has to be understood at the identity level.

At the heart of this book is a five-part Lawyer Career Satisfaction Model℠ that you can use as a lens to look inside your own career identity. Once you identify the five core elements of your identity, you will be much better equipped to identify jobs—and careers—that will fit who you are, whether that's in law or in some other field. This approach works well for all kinds of transitions. And whether you plan to stay in law, move to a law-related job, or leave law far behind, the same approach of clarifying your own identity first will prove to be a winning strategy. The best part is that because you will be focusing on your identity—that is, your essential self that remains constant throughout your lifetime—the criteria you identify by working through the exercises in this book are likely to remain valid for the remainder of your career even if you change jobs.

The Lawyer Career Satisfaction Model℠ will be introduced in Section II (Chapter 5), and the five chapters that follow will discuss the elements of the model and provide case study examples from actual clients. To protect identities, I have taken the liberty of combining the experiences of multiple clients into various "composite" profiles. The chapters in Section II (and Appendix D) contain exercises that I field-tested with actual clients, and I can assure you that the exercises really work (but you actually have to do them in order to benefit). I have found that one of the most successful strategies for effective career identity clarification is repetition. That is, if you complete one exercise—for example, to identify your core values—you will gain a little bit of insight about yourself. But if you do three or four or even five different activities—all aimed at clarifying your career values—you will begin to see patterns that give you a much higher level of confidence that you're on the right track. For this reason, it's important that you do all the exercises in the book, not just the first of each type. It would be easy to say to yourself, "Hey, I've already done this one," and move on. Don't rob yourself of the richness and clarity of doing them all.

Once you have identified the elements of your career identity, I will show you how to identify your job criteria and ideal job, and how to successfully navigate the job search and transition process. I'll also provide you with some additional resources for further exploration.

To get the greatest value from this book, I also suggest that you work through the chapters sequentially. They've been organized in order of the most important elements first. Still, for those readers who prefer to work through the chapters at random, each chapter has been written as a self-contained lesson so that you can still benefit. But, again, I do recommend a sequential approach if you want to enjoy the maximum benefit.

CHAPTER 2

Why This Book Was Written (and for Whom)

This book grew out of my experience as a career counselor for lawyers.

I come from a family of lawyers, and I practiced law myself for 10 years …but finally had to admit to myself that I didn't enjoy it. At one point, I went to a career counselor who gave me a battery of tests and declared that I should be a lawyer. I explained that I *already* was a lawyer and didn't like it. And when I told him that I wanted to do something different, he tried to convince me that I was mistaken. Putting aside the fact that he was probably not a very good counselor, my experience led me to take the career counseling process into my own hands.

I did a lot of research about career development in the hope that somehow I would be able to figure out what else I could do with my law training. Along the way, a funny thing happened: I grew to like the very process of career counseling. I found it interesting and rewarding to realize that there were models and strategies that could help people clarify their career direction. More importantly, I realized that I was going about the career search process all wrong. I had assumed that the most important question to answer is *"What jobs are out there?"* From my research, I became convinced that it's far more important first to clarify your own career identity and then, with that clarity, to look for or create a job that fits who you are. This idea of a "job-person fit," it turns out, is thoroughly supported by modern vocational research. It's the proven approach that leads to greater job satisfaction in the long run.

After all my research, I concluded that I liked helping people and decided to earn a Ph.D. in psychology. Simultaneously, I slowly began my own career counseling practice limited just to lawyers seeking greater career satisfaction. My counseling practice grew, and eventually I quit practicing law altogether and just did career counseling. Ultimately, I switched to doing consulting work for law firms, helping them with their "people" issues. But my experience in counseling lawyers has always given me a solid understanding of what the experience is like for a lawyer in practice, particularly lawyers working in traditional law firms.

These days, most of my practice is devoted to management consulting for law firms. But having spent over 15 years counseling lawyers, I realized that, through trial and error, I had developed a useful model that might benefit others. Tanya also experienced dissatisfaction practicing law. After working for a firm for four years, she knew that law wasn't a good fit, but didn't know what was. She had read many career books, looking for guidance as to what she should do next. She didn't find what she was looking for, but what she *did* find was inspiration to write a book herself. Her idea was for a career guidance book, just for lawyers, to help them find the best job for them based on their personality and other internal factors. Her research led her to some of my articles on the lawyer personality. She proposed collaboration, and our partnership was born.

Who in particular might benefit from this book?

I'm sure there are many different kinds of people who might find this information useful, but these are the groups of individuals I had in mind as I wrote this book:

- Out-of-Work Lawyers, page 5
- Dissatisfied or Burned-Out Lawyers, page 6
- Law Students and Recent Graduates, page 6
- Retiring or Senior Lawyers, page 7
- Career Counselors and Coaches, page 8

Out-of-work lawyers

Your predicament. You don't have a law job and you can't find one. There have been many casualties of law firm layoffs in this economy. Current law firm hiring is sluggish or frozen. You might be frustrated that you can't find work as a lawyer, or you might be relieved that you don't have to go back to your old job.

The opportunity. If you are unemployed, you probably don't have the luxury of waiting around for something to land in your lap, or of being indecisive about your future. Unhappy lawyers who have jobs may never figure out what they would rather be doing. You, on the other hand, must take focused action.

What you need. Direction…fast.

How this book can help you. This book is a practical, do-it-yourself, beeline path to clarity about your career. The insight you gain from this book will guide you as you decide which positions to apply for; making sure that you go after only opportunities that are a good fit for you. It will also provide you a benchmark to evaluate job offers and inform your decisions. Most important, when you start by clarifying who you are and what you need, you find that your job search actually gets easier. As a result, you will convey greater confidence and clarity of direction, qualities that employers find attractive in a job candidate.

Dissatisfied or burned-out lawyers

Your predicament. You have a law job but you don't like it. Or, at least, you're not sure it's the right long-term choice for you. Lawyers who find themselves in this category run the gamut from mildly bored, unfulfilled, and wondering *"Is this all there is?"* to completely miserable: *"I would quit today if I knew what to do next."* Whether you are an associate questioning your career choice, or an experienced partner feeling bound by golden handcuffs (or, more likely these days, silver), even if you know you want to do something else, you might not know what that is (and think it would be crazy to let go of a job in this economy).

The opportunity. You have the chance to discover your true career identity while still working...and then to put a plan in place to make necessary changes. You also get the opportunity to realize that it's not asking too much to be satisfied in your job, and it is possible. Others have found it; you can, too.

What you need. You know that something's wrong, but what? You need a method to systematically analyze the various elements of your career identity so you can change exactly what isn't working—no more and no less.

How this book can help you. Until now, there hasn't been a reliable, proven way to figure out exactly what isn't working in your job or career. This book will provide just that. With the knowledge you gain here, you might not need to "throw the baby out with the bath water". You will have the confidence that you are making the right change for you, based on your true career identity.

Law students and recent graduates

Your predicament. You may or may not yet have a job, but, in either case, you're still not sure what kind of job is right for you. Worse still, the current legal job market is the toughest in 80 years. Jobs are scarcer and more competitive; associate compensation models are beginning to change; and a legal education no longer provides the automatic path to partnership and profits it once did. Maybe that's just fine with you, if you never intended to practice anyway. More and more law students are opting out of the traditional law firm experience, whether by choice or necessity. But there is no single, clear-cut career path for those who want to use their law degree in nontraditional ways. Whether you feel resentful, confused, optimistic, or all of these, it's clear that this is not your grandfather's legal profession.

The opportunity. Change, whether welcome or not, always create new opportunities. Some avenues may close, but new ones are being paved right now, and possibilities for the future are still being dreamed up. The world is open to you when it comes to using your legal education in new and imaginative ways. Now is the perfect time for you to chart your course, rather than just drifting from job to job, only to wake up a couple of decades later wondering what happened.

What you need. A compass...and inspiration.

How this book can help you. It will show you how to discover the one critical thing law school didn't teach you—your unique career identity. This, in turn, will show you where to channel your legal education and interest in the law for the greatest career satisfaction. By seeing what's possible for you and where you best fit into the world of work, you can light or rekindle your excitement about your future.

Retiring or senior lawyers

Your predicament. You are facing the end of your career, but you aren't sure what's next. You've had a long legal career, with its ups and downs. You've no doubt accomplished many of your professional goals. But when contemplating retirement, you might be feeling a nagging sense of loss or something missing. Maybe you need to work longer for financial reasons, but you don't necessarily want to practice law anymore, at least not full-time. You would like some more flexibility in your life, and the chance to do something, well, different.

The opportunity. You have the golden opportunity to carve out a rewarding second career for yourself, to create your life as you want it to be, to contribute to the next generation in a meaningful way, if that's what you'd like to do, and to leave a lasting legacy.

What you need. A purpose—not just any old job to fill the hours or bring home a paycheck, but one that makes a difference in others' lives and your own.

How this book can help you. It will show you how to translate not only your wealth of experience, but also who you are, at your very core, into the next phase of your life, which could be the very best yet.

Career counselors and coaches

Your predicament. Your job entails counseling lawyers about career issues, and you're not always sure exactly how to advise them. If you are a generalist, you probably see your share of lawyer clients. More than most careers, lawyers identify very strongly with their profession. For many, being a lawyer defines them. There is even a distinct "lawyer personality." As a result, it can be particularly devastating and disorienting if they find that it's not working out as they had planned, for whatever reason.

The opportunity. If you understand what type of people go into the law, what drives lawyers, and the kinds of environments in which they find themselves working, you will be much more successful in counseling and coaching them, particularly around the career issues for which so many lawyers seek guidance.

What you need. The inside scoop—a book written by lawyers, about lawyers, for lawyers—to take you behind the scenes and inside the legal mind, unlocking the keys to their career identity.

How this book can help you. It will give you composite profiles of actual lawyers who made career changes—showing their transitions and illustrating how the book's principles work in real life. It will give you a roadmap, a blueprint for guiding your lawyer clients through the career change or planning process to a more satisfying job.

What this book offers to all of these types of individuals, and perhaps others, is an opportunity to systematically look within at who you are, what gives you satisfaction, and to explore the other key criteria that will influence your long-term career satisfaction.

CHAPTER 3

The Nature of Transition

Author William Bridges discusses at length the nature of career transitions in his classic *Transitions: Making Sense of Life's Changes* (and a later work, *Managing Transitions: Making the Most of Change*).

If you are familiar with this relatively short, but insightful piece of work, you know that transitions consist of an ending, a middle…and then a new beginning. The middle phase is called the neutral zone. Some ancient cultures understood the importance of the neutral zone and embraced it with formal rites of passage. Western culture doesn't acknowledge it very much, and seems to be uncomfortable with spending too much time there. Witness the people who have lost a job, loved one, or relationship, and who are encouraged by well-intentioned others to get "back in the saddle," and get on with their lives as soon as possible. It's almost as though others are as uncomfortable with our uncertainty as we are.

Too often we grasp at the next thing that comes along because we're so uncomfortable with the unknown. We feel "naked" without a professional label. When you decide it's time to discard one particular label, or if it has been discarded for you, you want to choose another one as quickly as possible. If we try to jump from Job A to Job B without any real reflection, we may make an external change, but no real inner shift has occurred. And a change made without the benefit of time spent in careful thought may result in an equally unsatisfying new job.

If we resist the neutral zone's rightful place at the center of a major transition, we also might miss out on the opportunity it offers. The seeds of the new beginning are sown here. This is the fertile ground for ideas that spark transformation. *Possibility lives in the neutral zone.*

We would do ourselves a great service to embrace the neutral zone. It's a tall order. You don't have to love this period of uncertainty. Just try to resist it a little less. Your main challenge during this time will be to expand the amount of discomfort you can tolerate. Stretch yourself just a bit more…and then a bit more. It isn't the end of the world. True, part of your world may be ending, but you will survive. And if you ask yourself what you can learn from the experience, you will undoubtedly discover things about yourself you didn't know. And you will realize that you are strong, that you can handle this, and that you will be okay.

Everyone's experience is a bit different.

I can't tell you how long to spend in the neutral zone. But I can tell you how to speed up the process.

You will need to start spending some regular, quality time by yourself. I realize that not everyone can take a sabbatical or even a vacation alone. But if you want to accelerate the process of making a new beginning, you will need to start stealing a few quiet moments here and there. If you are unaccustomed to spending time alone, it may feel awkward and uncomfortable, even selfish, at first. Practice in small increments.

You will also need to start listening to your gut instincts. Either by nature or by training, or both, lawyers tend to be a very logical, left-brained group and very skilled at using the rational side of their brain to make decisions. They make lists of pros and cons. But determining your next step on the way to career satisfaction is not—cannot be—solely an intellectual decision. If you analyze career choices the way you would a legal problem, you may very well end up in another career that challenges your mind but doesn't fulfill you. Stop looking around you for the answer, because even if it's staring you in the face, you won't recognize it unless you've first looked inward.

Dealing with Uncertainty

There will probably be times when you will feel like giving up. Don't. Making any kind of major life transition is difficult. People don't generally like to be pushed very far outside their comfort zones. It's scary. It's unpredictable. It's the unknown. You feel out of control. People in general—and lawyers in particular—like to feel in control of their lives. Making a major career shift—especially when so much of your identity has been invested in your job—is especially challenging. Even just considering the idea of such a major change can send some people running back to the safety of what feels familiar. There is no sugar-coating it.

For some people, just facing the reality that their chosen profession is not what they thought it would be sends shock waves through their whole life. It can feel like your foundation has been ripped out from under you. If you are one of those people who always wanted to be a lawyer and never really considered doing anything else, your disillusionment can seem like the death of a dream. You may begin to question everything, and it might seem like nothing is sure anymore. You second-guess yourself and question your judgment. If you got this wrong—such a big, important decision in life—what else might you be wrong about? Do you really even know yourself anymore or what you want?

It's no wonder that most people struggle with making a major change. Indeed, given human nature, it would be strange if it came easy to people. We shouldn't be surprised, but somehow it seems more difficult than we thought it would be. You can make it a bit easier on yourself, though, if you understand the stages of transitions and accept each stage as a necessary part of the process.

Don't worry. Others have been through this before. We tend to over-catastrophize and worry about the negative. It's human nature. It's normal to think about the worst possible case, but it's not likely to happen. The neutral zone doesn't last forever, and people make transitions all the time. If you do all the exercises in this book, you will probably have a good idea of the direction you want to go. But until you actually try it out and implement your plan, you won't know whether it really feels right. That's okay, just take action. It's the only way you'll find out, and you can always correct your course along the way. It may take awhile to complete your transition, but when you've reached your goal, you will be able to look back and see how far you've come. The hard part will be behind you. And it will all seem totally worth it.

SECTION II
WHO ARE YOU?

Chapter 4   The Case for Self-Assessment   *14*

Chapter 5   Introducing The Lawyer Career Satisfaction Model℠   *17*

Chapter 6   Does Your Job Fit Your Values?   *31*

Chapter 7   Does Your Job Fit Your Psychological Needs?   *49*

Chapter 8   Does Your Job Fit Your Communication Style?   *57*

Chapter 9   Does Your Job Fit Your Motivated Skills?   *69*

Chapter 10   Does Your Job Fit Your Career Interests?   *80*

CHAPTER 4

The Case for Self-Assessment

At this point, you might still be wondering why you should read this book and do all the exercises. In fact, you might be tempted to turn to Appendix A (*800+ Ways to Use Your Law Degree*), and research a few areas that look interesting. That's understandable, but it *won't* work. You won't find what you're looking for—career satisfaction—in a list of jobs. Not until you first identify the elements of your *career identity*.

I want to begin this chapter with a story. It's a story about a lawyer named Robert, who was a practitioner for some 20 years but who was depressed and hated his work.

At a career workshop for lawyers, Robert confided to the group the main reason he hadn't left the law. He said he had promised each of his sons that he would put them through college, and the only way he could afford to meet that commitment was to continue practicing. When one of the other lawyers asked if he shared that with his sons, Robert looked away. "I can't do that," he said softly, shaking his head. He had given his word, and that was that. Then something unexpected happened. Robert arrived at the next meeting looking 10 years younger and 100 times happier. He DID tell his eldest son about his career conflict, and was astonished at the young man's response. His son urged him to quit, saying that he admired his father for putting him through college, but that he and his brothers all wanted his father to enjoy the same opportunity to prove himself. More importantly, they all missed the supportive, fun-loving dad they had before Robert's depression set in.

Two years later, I ran into Robert at a CLE. He was wearing a bus driver's uniform, and had a big smile. It seems he left his partnership six months after the workshop ended. And now, he supports his family (and an interest in fiction writing), by driving a city bus, teaching in a paralegal program, and handling a little bit of legal work on a contract basis.

You might not have made the same choice, but it worked for Robert.

The point is, you don't have to turn to driving a bus to spend quality time with your family, or take a vow of poverty to find meaning in your work. But you do need to clarify what I call your *career identity* before you can bring your priorities and the realities of your life into alignment. And until you engage in some level of personal reflection—and self-assessment—you can't know how much you'll have to give up or whether the trade-off is worthwhile.

What Do You Want?

In a troubled economy, the what-do-you-want question might have limited appeal. At a time of legal restructuring, the more pressing questions might be **what** jobs are out there, **what** jobs can I get, **what** jobs come with a lawyer's stature, prestige, and income, etc? While there is inherently nothing wrong with these questions, they really won't help you find what you're looking for. Why? **Because career satisfaction occurs at the level of personal subjective experience.** For example, suppose I asked you, "What does career satisfaction mean to you?" and you said, *having a nice home, a decent income, and plenty of time to enjoy it.* These are external to you. They are *extrinsic rewards*, and—while desirable—extrinsic rewards won't get you any closer to achieving a genuinely satisfying job or career. In fact, if you are largely motivated by the extrinsic rewards of a job, you will come up short in your quest for satisfying work. But…if you told me that, for you as a lawyer, career satisfaction is all about *helping people*, or, *handling exciting assignments*, or, *spending a large part of each day engaged in intellectual dialogue with smart people*, I would say that by focusing on the intrinsic rewards you are a lot closer to understanding what sort of work you need to have a satisfying career.

OK, so what stands between you and a satisfying job or career?

The lawyer personality.

After all, there are certain personality traits common among lawyers; personality traits that help you to be a good lawyer. And the first place they may show up is in resistance to following the advice of a career book, and working through the recommended exercises. For example, if you're like most lawyers, you're skeptical (you need to be convinced that advice is worth taking)…you're autonomous (you don't like people telling you what to do)…you're impatient (you don't have the patience for self-exploration)…you're private (you dislike anything you consider "touchy feely")…and you may be defensive (you don't want to have it pointed out, or admit to yourself, that you might have chosen a career that is not a good fit for you). Altogether, these traits could pose significant barriers in your quest to find the right job.

It would be so much easier just to look at a list of jobs. And if that's what you really want, turn to Appendix A to find 800+ ways to use your law degree.

However, I believe that you are reading this book because you want to achieve true career satisfaction, and I have a proven method to help you do that. So, as you work your way through this book, continue to ask yourself, "What essential experience do I want as a daily part of my work?" and, "How do I want to feel when I do my work?" From one chapter to the next, your answers will go to the heart of learning your **career identity**...which is what really drives career satisfaction.

CHAPTER 5

Introducing the Lawyer Career Satisfaction Model℠

As I explained in Chapter I, career satisfaction is not about *"what's out there,"* but rather *"what's in here."* And for that, we need to take an inner-directed approach to career satisfaction. This chapter introduces the five elements of The Lawyer Career Satisfaction Model℠, after which an entire chapter will be devoted to each element, how they all fit together, and how you can discover your own satisfying career. Finally, in Section III, I will offer some recommendations about the job search and change process, and how to find the resources to assist you.

From this point on, each chapter will have important written exercises for you to do.

The most valuable insights are going to come from you. So, I strongly encourage you to spend some time reflecting on the questions and giving thoughtful answers. I compiled these exercises during my years as a career counselor to lawyers. They have helped many other lawyers in their self-discovery process, and they can help you, too, so try to complete all of them. If you invest time and energy into the process of self-assessment, you will be rewarded with greater self-knowledge. In turn, you will make more informed, enlightened decisions regarding your career.

One of the most frustrating parts about the experience of career dissatisfaction is not being able to pinpoint exactly what is wrong.

Maybe you can identify a few aspects of your job, or your firm, or the law that you dislike, but somehow these complaints don't capture the full measure of your discontent. Or maybe you have absolutely no idea where you got off track. Everything was going swimmingly for a while, and then one day you realize that the well has run dry, and what used to bring you professional pride and satisfaction is no longer fulfilling. You can't remember the last time you looked forward to going to work.

What should you do?

What can you do?

In our darkest hours, a complete and final break with the law can seem like the best option—or our only hope.

It can be very tempting at this juncture—when you're bored, confused, frustrated, disillusioned, depressed, or despairing—to want to chuck it all. Maybe escape to a fishing village in the Caribbean. Or open up that little shop you've been daydreaming about?

After you've completed the exercises in this book, maybe you will decide that you are better off working in an entirely different career, and that what you really want to do is restore an old farmhouse in France, travel the Texas Hold'em circuit, raise thoroughbreds, or launch a "green" technology company. I'm willing to bet, though, that most of you won't need to look so far out of your field to find happiness on the job. Because often, just a small or moderate change in your circumstances can make all the difference in your work experience. The challenge is to identify what you need to change.

The Lawyer Career Satisfaction Modelˢᴹ will help you do just that. If, on the other hand, you are not burned out or dissatisfied, but are just starting out or winding down a legal career, this model can help you, too. It will assist you in identifying exactly what type of legal or nonlegal career you want next.

A "Job-Person Fit" Model

The Lawyer Career Satisfaction Modelˢᴹ is what I call a "job-person fit" model. That is, it assumes that jobs are not good or bad in themselves, but that you will perceive or experience a job as "good" when you and your job are closely aligned. When we talk about *"job fit," we mean how congruently your career identity corresponds to the characteristics of the job.* When your job fits you, you will feel that your career identity is reflected in your work, and that your work is an extension of who you are. The result is a fulfilling work experience—in other words, career satisfaction.

It's true that every person's career identity is unique, but we can make some useful generalizations.

When we're talking about career identity for lawyers, we can think of a lawyer's identity as composed of the five basic elements—*Values, Psychological Needs, Communication Style, Motivated Skills, and Career Interests.* The more of these elements that fit your job, and the greater the congruence between each element and your job, the happier you will be. Values represent the greatest part of your career identity, followed by your psychological needs, your communication style, your motivated skills, and finally your career interests. Career interests, although important, exert a less powerful influence on career satisfaction than most other career guidance books would have you believe, especially for lawyers.

To achieve true career satisfaction, you need to take three steps:

Discover your career identity. This means understanding not only what you have to offer an employer, but also what you want and need in a work experience. Specifically, you must know what values, psychological needs, communication style, motivated skills, and career interests are most important to you.

Develop your job criteria. After you identify the elements of your career identity, you should be able to create a checklist of your own personal criteria for career satisfaction. You'll identify what you must have, what you'd like to have, and what you must avoid. Later, this checklist can be used to evaluate various job possibilities in general, as well as specific positions within particular firms or organizations during your job search.

Consider your circumstances. After you identify job possibilities that appeal to you, you may have to consider other factors such as geographical location, availability of jobs, need for further training, minimum required income, family needs and desires, and so on.

Don't expect to be struck with an epiphany overnight. At some point, you may find that everything seems to crystallize. More often than not, though, these moments of clarity will be the result of hours of thoughtful reflection and self-assessment. *In other words, doing the work.* But don't let this discourage you. The process will seem less daunting if you break it down into manageable tasks, as this book will show you how to do.

To begin, each of the five elements of your career identity—your values, your psychological needs, your communication style, your motivated skills, and your career interests—is associated with a diagnostic emotion.

When your values, needs, style, skills, or interests fit with a job, you typically experience a positive emotion; when there's a mismatch between the element and the job, you typically experience a negative emotion.

We will isolate and discuss the diagnostic emotions associated with each of five elements to help you determine whether the element fits your job or not. In later chapters, we will explore each element of your identity in greater depth. But for now, let's quickly look at some of your career emotions:

Career Element #1: Your Values

When personal values are not met in a job, the diagnostic emotion most people feel is disappointment. But when a value not only goes unmet but is actively violated, the emotion frequently experienced is anger. When values are fulfilled through a job, the emotions most people feel are satisfaction or fulfillment.

Values are self-maintained personal standards that are rooted in emotional life; they may or may not make logical sense. Think of them as positive likes or wants. Some examples of values commonly held by lawyers include intellectual challenge, interesting subject matter, variety, security, money, power, prestige, helping people, having an impact on society, balance between work and personal life, autonomy, and responsibility. Of course, these are only a few of the possible values, and you may find that your own values bear no resemblance to those of the "typical" lawyer.

Values can be quite specific or very global and abstract. On the more abstract end of the spectrum, the values become more assumptive and less conscious; that is, the value is taken for granted and assumed to be a universal truth—*"Wouldn't everyone agree with me that the more money the better?"* Values held at this level often are so deeply embedded that we can only learn what our specific values are from someone else who does not hold them, or from someone trained to identify them such as a psychologist or a career counselor, or from an exercise designed to uncover them.

One of the things this book will do is help you identify your deeply ingrained values. For example, if one of your values is helping people, and your boss is continually cheating people, you will likely feel very angry. Or suppose one of your values is being healthy. Working for a tobacco company would probably be offensive to you, and you'd be angry if your job required you to defend tobacco products.

Conversely, when values are fulfilled through a job, most people report experiencing a deep sense of satisfaction and fulfillment, often feeling as though they have "come home." These feelings are the sign that your job fits your values. The job feels "right." It feels like "you." In fact, it is an extension of you; your very identity is being validated through your work. For example, let's say you are an environmental lawyer and you take a job for Greenpeace, doing work that you believe in strongly. Every day you get up and you think, *"Wow! This is really what it's all about. I feel as though I've found my niche. Every day I do something that furthers what I'm about as a person."* These are the diagnostic emotions of someone whose job fits his or her values.

Values have an analog quality—they're like a dimmer switch. In other words, your job can fulfill your values to varying degrees; it's not all or nothing. Think of values as a continuum. How strongly you hold a particular value sets the "satisfaction point" along the continuum for that value. The more your job fits that value, the farther you move along the spectrum toward your satisfaction point. Example: let's say you value helping people. You could potentially find a job in which you help people a little bit, a job in which you help people a lot, and a job in which the entire job consists of helping people. Depending on where your satisfaction point lies for this particular value, one of these jobs is going to move you closer to your satisfaction point than the others.

Your values are the most important aspect of your career identity, because they explain about 80 percent of a lawyer's level of career satisfaction. So when you talk about identity, you're really talking about values. If you want to know what values someone holds, ask him or her, "What is important to you?" That is the classic value evocation question. The person will answer in the form of a value statement. "What's important to me about my job is...." Ask this question of yourself to begin thinking about what values you hold most strongly.

...AND WHAT'S IMPORTANT ABOUT THAT?

To really get to the root of what is important to you in a job, you will probably need to ask yourself this question—or have someone else ask it of you—several times in order to "drill down" to the bottom-line value. For example:

Q: "What's important to me in a job?"
A: "I want to work fewer hours."

Q: "And what's important about a job with fewer hours?"
A: "I'd have more free time."

Q: "And what's important about free time?"
A: "I could spend more time with my family."

Q: "And what's important about spending time with family?"
A: "That's what life is all about."

In this example, the last response finally arrives at what is really important to this individual: work-life balance. Try this exercise yourself or with someone else. Repeat the question until you can't come up with another reason why you want something—you just want it. When you don't have another answer for "…*and what's important about that?*" you know you have arrived at a bottom-line value.

Career Element #2: Your Psychological Needs

When a psychological need is met, you usually feel nothing at all. But when a psychological need is not met, the diagnostic emotion is frustration and a sense of urgency, and you're suddenly very interested in getting that need met. Failure to identify psychological needs often results in an unsatisfactory job or career change.

Unlike a value, a **psychological need** is a compelling drive that operates unconsciously. While a value can be conceptualized as a positive and desirable aspect of a job, a need is closer to a psychological hunger for a certain experience. Some of the more common psychological needs include the needs for power or control, affection, intimacy, inclusion in a group, approval, precision, continuity, security, effectiveness, closure, connection, openness, and predictability. These and other needs are held internally in some sort of rough hierarchy. The needs on the higher end of the hierarchy are the ones that must be met at all costs.

You may not value a particular need of yours. You may even hate that you have this need. But a need may exert an influence whether you like it or not. It must be met or you will suffer psychologically. Example: imagine a person who doesn't like that he or she needs intimacy. The person would like to be a stoic and go through life on his or her own. But the person realizes his or her need for intimacy, contact, and connection with other human beings, even though he or she values individualism. Those needs must be met, despite the person's independence. Another example: let's say you work in a firm in which you report to a partner who is controlling and manipulative. If you have a high need for control (as is common with many lawyers), you are likely to experience a great deal of frustration in working with this partner on an ongoing basis. You may not even connect your frustration to a specific event, but you will feel it nonetheless. So if you're frustrated in your job, there's a good chance one or more of your needs is not being met.

Usually, when one of the five career elements results in a good fit between you and your job, it produces a positive emotion. The psychological need category is the one exception to this principle. When a need is met, you usually feel nothing at all—the awareness of the need recedes into the background, and you focus your attention on other things. In other words, meeting the need makes the negative emotion disappear, but a positive emotion rarely takes its place. The need becomes invisible. This effect is similar to what happens when a physiological need is met—breathing air isn't likely to give you any noticeable sense of satisfaction unless you have been deprived of it. Contrast this experience with a value, which does lead to a positive emotion when it is met.

Whereas values operate on a dimmer switch, psychological needs operate more like an off-on switch—they're digital rather than analog.

A need either is met or it's not.

If you have a need that is not met, it trumps your values until it is met. Let's take a physiological need as an example. You have a need for oxygen. Right now that need is met. You are not thinking about how much you enjoy air. In fact, you're not thinking about air at all because you're getting your respiratory needs met. Let's imagine, however, that someone hooks up a big vacuum pump to your room or office and sucks out all the air. You would suddenly become very interested in getting air, and everything that otherwise holds your attention would pale in comparison until your air was restored. So it is with psychological needs. Because psychological needs that are met are usually invisible, it is easy to overlook your needs that are being met in your current job.

Consider the lawyer who's looking for a new job.

The lawyer looks for a position that fits his or her values, skills, and interests. The lawyer thinks that he or she has made an informed career choice, takes the jump from Job 1 to Job 2, and then is surprised and bewildered when he or she is frustrated with her new position just three months into the job. What happened? Job 2 looked so good from the perspective of Job 1. What the lawyer didn't realize is that Job 2 fails to meet a fundamental need that Job 1 met. Because the need was previously met, it wasn't on the lawyer's radar screen, and therefore he or she didn't include it in the career identity analysis.

Because your needs are largely unconscious, it is vital that you identify the primary needs responsible for your individual satisfaction, make them conscious and explicit, prioritize them, and learn how specific job roles are likely to meet or frustrate those needs.

Career Element #3: Your Communication Style

When your communication style doesn't fit the work you do, or the people with whom you work, it creates the diagnostic emotion of confusion or alienation. When your preferred style of communication does fit the prevailing style in your workplace, the most common emotion experienced is a sense of camarade-rie and congruence.

We all develop patterns in the way we interact with people, deal with data, make decisions, schedule events, and adopt a range of other behaviors. These patterns of behavior have been classified into recognizable styles by a number of theorists. By understanding these models of **communication style**, you can draw some important conclusions about the types of people you'll enjoy working with, the kinds of tasks you're likely to enjoy, and the variety of information you'll prefer dealing with. One of the most popular models of this type is Carl Jung's Theory of Psychological Types. A number of tools measure the personality preferences that Jung identified, but the best-known and most widely used is the Myers-Briggs Type Indicator (MBTI). The MBTI measures preferences along four basic dimensions:

- **Extraversion vs. Introversion** (where you prefer to focus your energy: externally or internally)
- **Sensing vs. Intuition** (what type of data you prefer to gather: factual, certain data, or global, impressionistic data)
- **Thinking vs. Feeling** (how you prefer to make decisions: based on objective logic or on subjective likes and wants)
- **Judging vs. Perceiving** (how you relate to people and data: in an organized, meticulous, and scheduled way or in a spontaneous, flexible, and informal way)

An individual whose communication style is mismatched at work feels like a fish out of water. You might think to yourself, "*What's going on here? It seemed like a good job, but something is not quite right. I can't stand what I'm doing, even though I like the people and it's a prestigious job.*" Or, "*I like the work, but the people here are just weird—they're definitely not my type.*" People become puzzled when everything else about the job seems right, but their preferred way of approaching tasks, relationships, decisions, or information doesn't match the accepted style for those things at work. The reason is that people usually don't have labels for their communication style. And when you don't have a label for something, you don't really see it. You just know that the job doesn't feel right.

On the other hand, if your preferred communication style does fit the prevailing style in your workplace, you could find yourself thinking, "*People here think like me. They talk like me. This is my kind of work.*" You feel a sense of common ground.

Knowing where you belong on the four MBTI dimensions (*extraversion/introversion*, etc.) can help you understand which kinds of work experiences are likely to give you pleasure, and which are likely to cause you dissatisfaction:

Extraversion vs. Introversion. *Extraverts* enjoy a workplace where they can interact with other people and where it's normal to "think out loud." *Introverts* probably feel a bit over-stimulated in that culture. They want a quieter work environment in which they can think through ideas before discussing them. For many introverts, it is important to manage the amount of external stimuli to which they are exposed. For example, it can be mentally exhausting for some introverts to spend a lot of time in meetings with others. They need some down-time to recharge their mental "batteries." Extraverts, by contrast, enjoy opportunities for external stimuli.

Sensing vs. Intuition. These two preferences represent different ways of gathering information about one's environment. *Sensing* types are more comfortable paying attention to specific, concrete, practical, realistic, and unambiguous details. They like paying attention to things in the here-and-now (or sometimes in the past), because in both time-frames they can be more certain about what's being perceived. *Intuitive* types, by contrast, are more comfortable paying attention to the big picture, to abstractions and possibilities, to broader trends, including how specific details weave together to form patterns. Intuitives like to focus on patterns, trends, themes, and the synthesizing process. They are more comfortable with abstractions and with the future time-frame. People with a sensing preference usually like to work with detail, while those with a preference for intuition generally enjoy working with more abstract concepts. If you're a sensing type and your job requires you to deal with "big picture" strategic issues, or if you're an intuitive and your job is to research the Tax Code, you're going to experience a mismatch between your style and your work.

Thinking vs. Feeling. These two dimensions measure the different ways of arriving at conclusions or making decisions. *Thinkers* value dispassionate, objective, detached, analytical logic, while *Feelers* value more personal, subjective, values-based choices. It's not that Thinkers don't have emotions—everyone does—it's just that their decision-making orientation favors rational analysis over subjective factors. Indeed, Feelers pay more attention to idiosyncratic differences, so-called "people" issues, and the impact of a decision on others. And they prefer a more harmonious approach to making decisions. It will come as no surprise that well over 75 percent of all lawyers prefer Thinking as their preferred decision-making style. This is a significantly larger proportion than the approximately 50 percent of the public who prefer Thinking.

Judging vs. Perceiving. This dimension measures whether you mainly prefer to gather data ("Perceiving") or make decisions ("Judging"). *Perceivers* are not any more perceptive than *Judgers,* and Judgers are not necessarily judgmental. Those with a Judging preference like to "cut to the chase", and they only want enough information to make a decision. By contrast, those with a Perceiving preference like to gather lots of information, and may wish to hold off on a decision until they can assess all their options. In other words, Judgers want closure while Perceivers want to keep their options open; Judgers tend to be organized, orderly, planned, and methodical, while Perceivers tend to be spontaneous, impulsive, open-minded, and flexible.

Career Element #4: Your Motivated Skills

> *When you don't get to use skills that you are good at and enjoy using, the diagnostic emotion you may feel is emptiness; the feeling that something is missing. When your job requires you to use skills that you are good at but don't enjoy using, it produces the diagnostic emotion of tedium. On the other hand, when your job allows you to use those skills that you both like and perform well, the diagnostic emotion you are likely to experience is effectiveness.*

Are you one of those people who went into law because you were always told, "You're so good at arguing" or, "You have such an analytical mind" or, "You're such a good writer…researcher…problem-solver…etc."? Those statements typify a person who has a strong skill in one of the things that lawyers typically do well. *But being "good" at something is only half of the equation. A part of your job satisfaction comes from doing something well that you also enjoy, that is, a motivated skill.*

In response to any of the above statements, the lawyer should ask himself or herself, "Do I like to argue? Do I like to write? Do I actually like to use this skill?" Most people who followed a path to law school based on the well-meaning suggestions of others never asked themselves the introspective question, "How do I feel about using that skill?" Instead, they simply asked the more analytical question, "Am I good at it?" If the answer is yes, the lawyer reasons that he or she should pursue it and ends up building a career on the basis of one skill—a skill the lawyer doesn't necessarily even enjoy using.

Don't get me wrong. Competence is important. But developing competence in skills you don't enjoy using is like climbing the career ladder only to discover that your ladder is propped against the wrong wall. If you begin with the skills you enjoy using, and work to develop competence in those areas, you will be much more likely to find job satisfaction from this element.

Motivated skills is a compound element: When this element is not met, two different kinds of job dissatisfaction are possible. First, the lawyer who becomes good at something he or she doesn't enjoy can easily become an expert at it in the law without really wanting to. For example, Kim was asked by a senior lawyer in her firm to proofread a brief he had written. She caught a couple of typos and suggested some stylistic revisions to clarify his argument. He was very appreciative, and mentioned it to the other partners. In time, other lawyers in the firm began coming to her, asking if she would just "look over" their documents before they were sent out. Since they were mostly partners, Kim didn't think she was in a position to say no. Before she knew it, she was the designated "proofreader" at the firm even though she didn't really want to be.

People who are stuck doing something they're good at but don't like often have the subjective experience of tedium. Doing the work feels like drudgery. Suppose you're great at arguing, but you're a healer not a fighter. You can do it when called upon, but who wants to? The first time you won a debate, everyone said you showed such great skill at verbal jousting that you really should be a lawyer. Then you went into law and you got positive reinforcement for arguing because you were good at it. Before you know it, you are inundated with work you don't want to do.

The other way in which a motivated skill can lead to dissatisfaction is when you don't get to use skills you are good at and enjoy using. Let's say you're proficient in and passionate about a second language, but your job doesn't call for you to use that language. You might feel as though you are missing a big part of what should be your work experience. The lack of opportunity to use skills that you enjoy can leave you feeling incomplete, as though a part of your identity is lying dormant. This kind of dissatisfaction can be even more demoralizing than the former. In contrast, when your job allows you to use those skills that you both like and perform well—i.e., *your motivated skills*—then the diagnostic emotion you are likely to experience is effectiveness.

Career Element #5: Your Career Interests

When a career interest is met, you feel interested; when it is not met, you feel bored.

The most visible of the five elements of career identity is your set of **career interests**—the topical areas of work that interest you. In law, this element would encompass the substantive practice areas that attract you. For example, are you interested in real estate? Health care? Taxation? Labor? In other occupations, the interest element might include the kinds of persons or entities you work with (e.g., animals, athletes, farmers), the kinds of products or services you deal with (e.g., telecommunications equipment, insurance, travel, finances, sporting goods), or the subject matter that you learn about (e.g., art, history, economics, politics).

While your career interests are certainly important, for most lawyers they are not as important as your values or psychological needs in determining your overall long-term career satisfaction. *However, because interests are the easiest items to test for, categorize, and conceptualize, they are often overemphasized in self-help books as the key to unlocking your best career path.* It is still possible to be miserable in your job even if the nature of your work is interesting. There is a lot more to job satisfaction than just matching your interests to the job. True job satisfaction must also take into account the other four career elements—values, psychological needs, communication style, and motivated skills.

Perhaps another reason that most career guidance books emphasize interests over the other elements discussed in this book is that these books are written for the population at large. However, studies have shown that people who do knowledge work—among them, lawyers—pay much more attention to intrinsic criteria in rating their satisfaction levels than to extrinsic criteria such as interests, which can and do change over the course of one's work life. Jobs that draw on intellect and judgment typically attract people who are satisfied primarily by the first four elements of The Lawyer Career Satisfaction Model℠.

Interests are still an important piece of the puzzle, but you need to be sure to accord them the proper weight compared to the other elements in the model if you want to achieve job satisfaction. That is, keep them in perspective. The diagnostic emotions associated with the satisfaction of this element are quite simple: interest or boredom.

Your Ideal Job

One dimension of The Lawyer Career Satisfaction Model℠ is career identity, and the other is "your ideal job". What is your ideal job? *It is the job that is congruent (fits) with the personal criteria this book will help you identify.* And to understand how a job "fits" your values, psychological needs, communication style, motivated skills, and your career interests, you must consider two aspects of a job—the nature of the job itself, and the job conditions and environment in which you work.

The type of job. First, you will need to determine the type of job that best fits your career identity. As a legal professional, you can choose from three categories: law jobs, law-related jobs, and non-law jobs (see Chapter 11). The type of job you do refers to the job tasks or job description. For example, if one of the criteria you value is "work/life balance," you can probably eliminate most large law firms with very high billable hour requirements and no flexibility in arrangements for individual lawyers (unless you find a firm with a meaningful work/life balance program or alternative career tracks). For many lawyers, work/life balance value may be more compatible with an in-house counsel position or with a position as a lawyer in a university, social or trade organization, or other setting where billable hours are not a factor in compensation. Identifying which jobs meet your criteria list can be quite complex, especially if your list contains competing criteria (such as potentially conflicting values: "make lots of money" versus "work part-time").

The job conditions and environment. Your choice of job category and type of job will not be the end of your search for career satisfaction. In fact, it may not even be the most important step. Career research indicates that for about 90 percent of lawyers, the primary source of job satisfaction comes from something other than identifying the right line of work or job category. You will need to find the right set of specific elements of the total work experience, many of which exert a strong influence on job satisfaction, no matter what type of job you do. For example, if you are one of those individuals for whom autonomy contributes the largest part of your job satisfaction, the specific kind of job you perform to afford you this autonomy is likely to be less of a factor than the autonomy itself.

So the working conditions or job environment become a second important factor to evaluate when you are trying to find a fit between your career identity and a particular job. Even if you have identified the type of job you think will interest you and use your motivated skills, you still need to make sure that your values and communication style will fit the "personality" of the firm or company you choose and that your psychological needs will be met. Often these latter factors have little to do with the kind of job you choose and much more to do with conditions at a specific workplace, such as the individual to whom you report, the physical layout of your office, and the "culture" of the office in which you work.

You should now have a general understanding of the five basic elements that form your career identity. In the next several chapters, we will cover each element in greater depth, and you will begin to explore the elements of your own career identity. Let's begin with the first and most important element... your values.

CHAPTER 6

Does Your Job Fit Your Values?

In this chapter, you will be introduced to three ways to think about your personal values. Each will measure something slightly different and give you insight into this most critical aspect of career satisfaction. You will also be invited to complete some exercises—seven, to be exact—to identify your values. The exercises build on each other, so I recommend you do them in order. With this deeper understanding, you will have an enormous advantage when contemplating any career decision. You will move from a position of uncertainty and confusion to one of clarity and self-knowledge. It will let you evaluate any job offer or career transition with confidence that you can make the best decision for you.

Have you ever worked on a task—whether it was a project for work, volunteering, family, community, or a hobby—where you were totally into it? Completely absorbed, engaged, passionate, immersed? In the flow? Chances are that whatever you were doing, the task was aligned with a value you hold. A value is nothing more than something you find important. There is an emotional connection—a value feels completely aligned with who you are.

> *When your values are aligned with your work, it is more likely that you will find meaning in your work. Research shows that the more people experience their work as meaningful, the more satisfied they are and the more engaged they will be in their work.*

How many of the following statements can you identify with? If you are not currently employed, think of your most recent work experience as you consider the following statements:

- *I feel a deep sense of satisfaction and fulfillment in my job.*
- *When I think about my job, I feel as though I have "come home."*

- *My job feels "right."*
- *My job feels like "me."*
- *I feel as though I've found my "niche."*

These statements reflect the experience of someone whose job fits his or her values. But if none, or very few, of these statements resonate, your job is very likely mismatched with your one or more of your values. If that's the case, you might identify with one of the following statements:

- *When I think about my job, I feel disappointed.*
- *I sometimes feel angry about my job or when I am at work.*

The first statement reflects the experience of someone whose values are not being met in his or her job, and the second statement reflects the experience of someone whose values are being actively violated.

Since you are reading this book, there is a fairly good chance that you do not have a job that is a great fit with your personal values. But whether you identified more with the first or the second set of statements, your values are fulfilled (or not) to varying degrees. Values are not generally experienced as "all or nothing" criteria. Think of most values as falling along a continuum. *The more your job fits your values, the farther you move along the spectrum toward job satisfaction. Also, your job can fit some of your values but not others.*

Right now, think about how well you think your job fits your values. Make an "X" at the spot on the continuum below that represents your best estimate of your overall job-value fit. From left to right, the continuum is expressed by the following points: Extremely Violated/Unfulfilled; Somewhat Violated/Unfulfilled; Neutral; Somewhat Fulfilled; Extremely Fulfilled

L_____I_____I_____I_____I_____I_____I

The Worldview Model

The late psychologist Clare Graves developed a model that explains six different common values systems. His model—which I will call the *worldview model*—says that the complex set of assumptions that each individual holds about how the world works—your values system—acts as a filter, coloring how you experience the world. While some of the values systems mentioned may seem very obvious, they are quite invisible to the person whose everyday behavior is filtered through them. In other words, you take them so much for granted that you can easily forget that not everyone sees the world in the same way. This gives these values systems an added degree of power since they are strongly influencing you but you may be unaware of their pull on you.

EXERCISE #1. IDENTIFYING YOUR WORLDVIEW

Each of the statements below represents the primary belief or assumption of the six major worldview values systems in this model. Rank the following statements from 1 to 6, with 1 being the statement you most strongly identify with, and 6 being the statement you least identify with or most strongly reject.

___ *Belief System 1:* The world is mysterious and threatening, and safety and security are all-important.

___ *Belief System 2:* The world is a hostile, dog-eat-dog place, and strength is the key to staying alive and on top of things.

___ *Belief System 3:* Life has a purpose and an order, and there is generally one right way to be.

___ *Belief System 4:* It is possible to do better than others and to win, to set goals and achieve them, and people should be rewarded for performance rather than for seniority.

___ *Belief System 5:* Life is about living in harmony with others and experiencing the subjective feelings of being human, and collective actions are the way to reach both societal goals and meet individual needs.

___ *Belief System 6:* The world is a complex place, and chaos and change are natural states that humans can adapt to. Getting done what needs to be done—efficiently and competently—matter more than rules, red tape, or interpersonal pleasantries.

If you identified most strongly with Belief System 1, your primary worldview is most likely *Safety Driven*.

If you identified most strongly with Belief System 2, your primary worldview is most likely *Power Driven*.

If you identified most strongly with Belief System 3, your primary worldview is most likely *Order Driven*.

If you identified most strongly with Belief System 4, your primary worldview is most likely *Success Driven*.

If you identified most strongly with Belief System 5, your primary worldview is most likely *People Driven*.

If you identified most strongly with Belief System 6, your primary worldview is most likely *Process Driven*.

So what do these labels mean? Let's look at the kinds of behaviors you typically see from each values system and how they often show up in lawyers and law firm settings.

One or more of these systems may seem weird or irrelevant to you – that's to be expected. Your deeply held values systems will seem so normal to you that it's hard to imagine anyone seeing things differently. Values systems that you reject may seem weird or foreign because it's equally hard to conceive of anyone embracing them. But the person in the office down the hall from you may feel exactly the same way—about an entirely different set of values! You will probably recognize aspects of yourself in several of these values systems, but try to pinpoint the one or two top systems that are most like you. Conversely, it is also important to identify the values systems that are least like you, since a rejection of a values system signifies a belief in the opposite of that values system. The stronger your feelings of rejection, the stronger your opposite value…so you know what to *avoid* in a job.

Are you safety-driven (dependent)? The kinds of behaviors you might see in people operating out of *Safety Driven* beliefs include looking for guidance from a single authority figure who is seen as all-powerful. It also includes a tendency to be superstitious and to see events as being caused by forces outside one's self. People holding this values system tend to think in "tribal" terms—there is safety in numbers; our leader will look out for us; there is more "we" than "I." It is unusual to find lawyers who hold a Safety Driven values system as their primary belief system. Quite the opposite is actually true—many lawyers have a stronger-than-average emotional rejection of this values system. Not only do they fail to identify with the dependency themes, but they are actively repelled by them. One illustration of this point: You may have noticed yourself or colleagues placing a stronger-than-average emphasis on personal autonomy in the workplace. Some lawyers, especially earlier in their careers, do identify secondarily with this values system. This moderate affinity for the Safety Driven values system is exemplified by the young associate who is afraid to complete any work assignment without close supervision by a mentor.

Are you power-driven (autocratic)? The kinds of behaviors you might see in people operating out of *Power Driven* beliefs include self-reliance, toughness, a love of challenges, and an insistence on getting what one wants right now. Power Driven individuals often feel, "*If you're not for me, you're against me.*" These individuals can be quite impulsive and unpredictable, as well as positioned and strong-willed. Mature application of this values system produces a street-smart effective advocate. Immature application of this values system produces a temperamental, petulant, "two-year-old" mentality. In law firms, this is rarely the prevailing values system in the firm as a whole, but it is not uncommon to find a sprinkling of individual lawyers for whom the Power Driven values system is most dominant. This values system is often found among fiercely competitive litigators. Lawyers who embrace an "eat what you kill" mind-set often have a touch of this value.

Are you order-driven (traditionalist)? The kinds of behaviors you might see in people operating out of *Order Driven* beliefs include following the rules; working hard now for deferred rewards, and thinking in a logical, consistent, and rational way. Traditionalists are most comfortable working within traditional bureaucratic structures, such as the government, large corporations, or traditional law firms. Most Traditionalists have firm beliefs that there is "one right way" to do things, and they judge others by this criterion. For Traditionalists, one works hard and climbs the ladder rung by rung, earning promotions as you go by following the rules, being a company player, and keeping your head down. Many Traditionalists identify with some larger institution to which they belong and draw some of their identity from affiliation with that institution. This values system is the most widely held in the United States, and is easily the primary value for many lawyers. It is also the primary value for many law firm administrative staff including paralegals.

Are you success-driven (achiever)? The Achiever seeks to achieve success and material gain, and to live "the good life." Achievers believe that if they work hard toward a goal, they should be commensurately rewarded for reaching that goal. The kinds of behaviors you might see in people operating out of *Success Driven* beliefs include competitiveness, but exercised judiciously so as not to alienate others. The Achiever sets long-range goals and moves toward them and tends to be entrepreneurial. Achievers believe in high technology and progress, and are willing to experiment and bend the rules if it produces a win. The Success Driven values system is the central values system of many U.S. businesses. More and more we are seeing this value emerge within the legal profession as firms shift from purely professional enclaves to methodically run businesses. The conflict between Traditionalists and Achievers is common because so many people in the legal profession believe in one of these two values systems. A handful of individuals value both systems highly.

Case study #1. *John worked for an insurance defense firm. He used to enjoy practicing law, but over time he grew disenchanted. Regardless how many hours he put in on a case, and regardless whether he produced a great result for the client or not, he was compensated just the same. There was no reward—no incentive—to work extra hard because his firm employed a lock-step compensation model, with small, annual cost-of-living increases for everyone. It wasn't just about the money for John. He wanted to work within a system that valued productivity, creative thinking, and innovation. John had a lot of ideas, and he began to consider ways to dabble in technology on the side. Eventually, he invented an application for mobile devices that he brought to market with the help of an engineer. John found the process of launching a start-up business very exciting and fulfilling. He planned to invent more products so that he could eventually leave private practice and focus on his technology business full-time. John's core value was Success-Driven.*

Are you people-driven (humanist)? The kinds of behaviors you might see in individuals operating out of *People Driven* beliefs include building consensus; collaborating; smoothing over conflict to create harmony; sharing feelings; sacrificing one's own needs to make the group (your firm, your society, etc.) better; and tolerance for a range of differences in others, including different values systems. Some lawyers are drawn to the People-Driven values system as a secondary values system. It is less frequently found as a primary values system among lawyers. *There are many more Traditionalists and Achievers in law firms.* And a small number of lawyers reject this values system, seeing Humanist behaviors as inefficient and overly sentimental.

Case study #2. *There were no lawyers in Richard's family, nor had he ever met one growing up. In fact, Richard had no idea what lawyers actually did on a daily basis, and he wasn't exactly sure why he had gone to law school. Not surprisingly, Richard didn't do well in law school, and years later he was totally miserable as a business lawyer. He hated legal analysis, negotiating, drafting contracts. Everything about his career seemed wrong…but he was clear about one thing: he knew he wanted to help people. Richard was sensitive, warm, and tactful. An idealist, he completely identified with the Humanist worldview. But he didn't understand why, even though he genuinely wanted his legal career to work out, he was so deeply unhappy. It's possible that Richard might have found a niche within the law that would have been more satisfying for him, but it wasn't meant to be. Richard ended up leaving the profession. Richard's core value was People-Driven.*

Case study #3. *Susan, like Richard, was a very unhappy lawyer. She had begun her legal career with a desire to help families through the difficult legal* *and emotional times of separation and divorce. She was very passionate about family law but couldn't stand the adversarial nature of the practice area. It seemed that all she did was put out fires and deal with one combative client after another. Unlike Richard, though, Susan did not want to give up her idealism, and was determined to find a way to make it work within the law. So she founded one of the first collaborative law practices in the country, creating a more consensual process and harmonious environment in which to support families through the end of a marriage and beyond. Susan finally got to practice family law the way she had always envisioned it. Susan's core value was also People-Driven.*

Are you process-driven (pragmatist)? Pragmatists believe in looking at the big picture and using a "systems" view of things. They may think that the other values systems lack a sufficient answer to deal with the world's complexity. The kinds of behaviors you might see in people operating out of *Process-Driven* beliefs include highly autonomous and self-sufficient behavior; eclectic interests; competency-based functional decision-making. In other words, the Pragmatist is very practical, and wants to get the job done in whatever way that works. He or she is willing to adapt to a changing situation as needed. The Pragmatist places a high value on competence and quality and may be heard to say, *Lead, follow, or get out of my way.* Pragmatists enjoy having an impact on a larger system such as the entire firm, their community, their nation, or the planet. They see individual actions as part of a more complete greater whole and, as a result, they tolerate ambiguity more readily. Many lawyers are Pragmatists. It is not uncommon to find this values system in combination with Humanist or with Achiever, and occasionally with Traditionalist.

Case study #4. *Jack had a very successful litigation practice in a midsize law firm. More and more, though, he felt that something was missing in his work. His cases were interesting on an intellectual level, but he felt increasingly constrained by the bureaucratic nature of working in a firm. And he wanted to have more immediate impact; impact that he could see. He finally decided to leave the practice of law and become an independent consultant, teaching trial practice skills and coaching star litigators in larger firms. Through this transition, Jack took more control of his daily work experience, and was able to see the immediate results of his efforts on a much more regular basis…without any of the red tape. Jack's core value was Pragmatist.*

If you are still unsure about your worldview, or if you can't decide between several, another way to look at this model is to examine the "end value" or ultimate experience that people with these values systems are seeking:

The dependent's end value is . . . to feel safe and protected.

The autocrat's end value is . . . to feel in control and not taken advantage of.

The traditionalist's end value is . . . to achieve security and stability.

The achiever's end value is . . . to feel a sense of accomplishment.

The humanist's end value is . . . to serve humanity.

The individualist's end value is . . . to be and feel effective and get results.

Which end value resonates with you? What is the ultimate experience you are looking for? Take a few moments to write it down:

My end value is:

_____

My primary worldview values system is:

_____

My secondary worldview values system is:

_____

The Career Anchors Model

Edgar Schein, a professor at the MIT Sloan School of Management, has developed a useful model known as "Career Anchors" that offers insight into work values. According to this model, each individual has one bottom-line value that acts like a magnet attracting that person to a job. While more than one of these values may be appealing, only one is likely to have that *bottom-line quality.*

EXERCISE #2. IDENTIFYING YOUR CAREER ANCHOR

Each of the following words represents one of the eight Schein career anchors. Which of the following is most important to you in a work experience? Rank them from 1 to 8, with 1 being the anchor that most resonates with you, and 8 being the anchor that least resonates with you.

___ Security	___ Craft
___ Autonomy	___ Principle
___ Entrepreneur	___ Challenge
___ Management	___ Lifestyle

Let's look at the eight career anchors in greater detail and see how they show up in lawyers and law firm settings. As with the worldviews, you will probably recognize yourself in several of these anchors, but try to pinpoint the top one or two that are most like you:

Security. *Your identity includes a need for security, predictability, or certainty.* This anchor can be obtained in two ways: geography and tenure. A geographical security anchor means that you meet your need for security by staying in one geographical area, with which you identify. A tenured security anchor means that you meet your need for security by staying with one law firm or company, with which you identify. A job as a partner in a conservative law firm that has been stable for more than 25 years might attract someone with a tenure type of security anchor. Any job within an easy commute of your identified geographical roots would likely meet your needs if your security anchor is of the geographical type. And if offered a better position in another part of the country, you would likely turn it down.

Autonomy. *Your identity includes a need for autonomy.* You want freedom from being controlled by other people. You may prefer to work on your own rather than for an organization. If you do work for an organization, you insist on a great deal of room to do your job your own way. You dislike rules. Creating your own law firm might be one way to maintain this value. Being the only lawyer in a small company might also serve you. Or simply having a lot of autonomy in your firm, e.g., due to having a big book of business, might do the trick.

Entrepreneurial. *You are driven by "building something creative."* Your identity is connected to the concept of taking an idea and developing it into a reality. Creativity is important. You like to have other people take care of the details so you can go on and develop more ideas. You like recognition. In law, people with an entrepreneurial anchor may create a unique practice or build their own law firm.

General Manager. *You like climbing the hierarchical ladder, making tough decisions, and managing people, capital, and information.* You care less about being loyal to one law firm or company than about moving upward. Someone with this anchor might grow into a managerial role in a law firm or parlay his or her legal experience into a position in the line management of a company.

Craft. *You already have identified with a particular skill, craft, or competency that you are good at and that you want to be better at.* You like to perfect your craft; indeed, you are the craft. You're someone who might say of themselves, "Who I am is a lawyer," as opposed to saying, "I practice law for a living." Only the former qualifies as a Craft anchor. This anchor is about loving your work for the intrinsic, rather than extrinsic, rewards it offers.

> **Case study #5.** *Greg was a litigator with a demanding caseload in a big firm with high billable-hour requirements. When he read the description of the Craft anchor, he said, "That's me. I have a craft. I'm a writer." He explained that every morning before going to the firm, he would think to himself, "I've written before, and I know I have it in me to write novels. I just need to get out of this sweatshop so I can do that." Greg had given up on the idea that writing was something he could do for a career. But through self-assessment, he came to realize that not using his craft was causing him stress at the identity level. In time, Greg transitioned to being a contract lawyer, and found that he had much more time and energy to get up in the morning to do what he needed to do... write.*

Principle. *You identify with a particular cause or principle, and it must be part of your work experience.* Your work actively furthers a principle that is important to you. You will quit an organization if it violates your personal values related to the cause. If protecting the environment is so important to you that it feels like part of your identity, for example, then this might be your anchor. You might do environmental litigation in a firm, work for Greenpeace, or even promote responsible reforestation within a paper company.

> **Case study #6.** *Elizabeth was an environmental litigator. Every time she had to go to court or argue with opposing counsel, it really upset her. Eventually, whenever she had to deal with conflict, she came to feel kind of dead inside. She was very ambivalent about continuing to practice law. But although Elizabeth found her work incredibly frustrating at times, she didn't want to give it up. Her sense of purpose and her values were validated in her work, and that outweighed her discomfort with the adversarial nature of her job. After assessing her career identity, Elizabeth came to realize that she was willing to tolerate conflict now and then in order to fulfill her sense of mission, which was a daily experience for her. Having looked at her situation with fresh eyes, Elizabeth was willing to accept this tradeoff.*

Pure Challenge. *You like adrenaline flowing in your veins. You are driven to be "the best," to compete (either against yourself or others), to be constantly challenged.*

You like testing yourself, pushing to "the edge." Professional athletes often embrace this anchor. It is less frequently found in law, although many litigators might identify with pure challenge, as well as corporate lawyers who love "doing deals."

Lifestyle. Work, for you, is just one way to balance all the elements of your life. You want a job that allows you enough time and money to enjoy your family, your friends, your hobbies, and your life. Work is not the most important thing to you. If this is your anchor, it is less important to specify the job that you do than to ensure that whatever you do does not interfere with the balance you have achieved, or want to achieve, in your personal life.

Case study #7. *Mike basically enjoyed practicing law but didn't like the long hours or the pressure to bring in clients. He had young kids, liked to exercise, and had several hobbies he wanted to pursue. He just wanted to do the work, be paid a reasonable salary, and go home in time to have dinner with his family. He also wanted his weekends free for social activities. Mike found a staff attorney position in a small government office. The work was predictable and not that exciting, but Mike was happy because it afforded him the work-life balance that was most important to him.*

Case study #8. *Stephanie was a very unusual—and dissatisfied—lawyer. The most important thing to her was to find a job that allowed her to be playful. As part of a traditional profession, most law firms are not exactly known for their playful work environments. Realizing that she would probably always experience a profound disconnect between her values and those of most legal employers, Stephanie decided to look for work outside the law. She began to explore unconventional options such as working and playing with kids in a hospital, and being a professional clown who is hired to inject a sense of levity at executive board meetings, and working as a professional storyteller.*

Case study #9. *Laura was a senior partner with a well-respected employment law practice. Although she worked in a midsized firm with a reasonable billable-hour requirement, Laura still found that her busy practice didn't leave much time for outside interests, especially while juggling child-rearing duties as a single parent. Rather than switch careers, Laura decided to continue practicing law, simplify her lifestyle, and create a savings and investment plan that allowed her to retire early. She moved from the city to a smaller community with a lower cost of living. She began a part-time encore career of winemaking, and still has time to read, write, visit friends and family, and travel.*

If you are still unsure which is your career anchor, one way to determine which value is your career anchor is to ask yourself, "If I am attracted to more than one, which is the last value that I would give up?" Alternatively, "Which one of these values comes closest to describing the 'real me'?"

If you can't decide which is your primary anchor, imagine that you could have all of one but none of the other, and vice versa. For example, if you can't choose between Autonomy and Entrepreneurial, imagine that you have all the autonomy in the world, but you are not allowed to create anything new. Conversely, imagine that you can create to your heart's content, but you have no autonomy whatsoever. This may be an extreme example and not a job you would choose in real life, but imagining the hypothetical situation and having to pick between two highly desired values forces the primary anchor to rise to the surface. What anchor do you not want to live without? Take a moment to write it down.

My primary career anchor is: _____

My secondary career anchor is: _____

Career Anchors: Self Assessment (3rd ed.), by Edgar H. Schein. Reproduced with permission of John Wiley & Sons, Inc.

The Values Card Sort Model

The Values Card Sort is another simple but effective tool to help you identify the values you most and least want in a job. It is a very tangible, interactive, and intuitive way to flush out your values and the priorities among those values. A deck of Values Cards is included in the book (see Appendix E). Each card contains a value that you might find attractive in the workplace.

EXERCISE #3. IDENTIFYING YOUR VALUES

1. Go to Appendix E. Cut out the pages and separate the cards. You should have a deck of 5 Category Cards and 48 Value Cards.
2. Place the five Category Cards (Always Valued, Often Valued, etc.) side by side horizontally.
3. Quickly sort all 48 Value Cards into the appropriate columns, placing those you would value most highly in an ideal job under the "Always Valued" column, and those values you would care less strongly about in the appropriate columns. Don't spend too much time analyzing the exercise; it works best if you sort as quickly as possible.

4. Now, rearrange the cards within each column so that they are ranked in priority order. In other words, your very strongest value will be at the top of "Always Valued," and your most detested value will be at the bottom of "Never Valued." Resist the temptation to arrange and rearrange several times; your first instinct is usually your truest. NOTE: You may not have more than eight cards in the "Always Valued" column.

5. When you are finished sorting, write down the values you selected in the exact order that your cards are laid out in each column.

Always Valued	Often Valued	Sometimes Valued	Seldom Valued	Never Valued
_____	_____	_____	_____	_____
_____	_____	_____	_____	_____
_____	_____	_____	_____	_____
_____	_____	_____	_____	_____
_____	_____	_____	_____	_____
_____	_____	_____	_____	_____
_____	_____	_____	_____	_____
_____	_____	_____	_____	_____

6. In two weeks, repeat the exercise…but without looking at the earlier results. It is very important that your second card sort be independent of the first. As before, write down the values in the exact order that your cards are laid out in each column.

Always Valued	Often Valued	Sometimes Valued	Seldom Valued	Never Valued
_____	_____	_____	_____	_____
_____	_____	_____	_____	_____
_____	_____	_____	_____	_____
_____	_____	_____	_____	_____
_____	_____	_____	_____	_____
_____	_____	_____	_____	_____
_____	_____	_____	_____	_____
_____	_____	_____	_____	_____

7. A minimum of two rounds of card sorting are necessary for this exercise. If you do a third sort, wait another two weeks before completing the exercise so you won't be influenced by the earlier results.

EXERCISE #4. CLASSIFYING YOUR VALUES

Look at the values you selected in your Always Valued column in both card sorts. Which values did you select both times? These are your **Primary Values**—deeply held and most important. The values that only showed up in this column in one of the card sorts are important, but less so. These are your **Secondary Values**. Write down your Primary and Secondary Values in the spaces below. It's also important to know which values you really dislike consistently. People tend to spend less time thinking about these, yet patterns emerge here just the same. The values you put in the **Never Valued** column in both card sorts should also be part of your personal roadmap as experiences to avoid. Write them down in the space provided.

Primary Values	*Secondary Values*	*Never Valued*
_____	_____	_____
_____	_____	_____
_____	_____	_____
_____	_____	_____
_____	_____	_____
_____	_____	_____
_____	_____	_____
_____	_____	_____
_____	_____	_____
_____	_____	_____

EXERCISE #5. PRIORITIZING YOUR VALUES

Look at your list of Primary Values. Compare them with your choices in the Always Valued columns (from both card sorts). Is there any one single Primary Value that was listed above all the rest in both card sorts? In other words, one value that rises above all others? If your Primary Values are in different order in the card sorts, look to see how their rankings relate to the other Primary Values in each card sort. The rankings may not work out perfectly, so it will be up to you to determine the ultimate priority of your values. Example: Suppose your first two card sorts yielded the following five Primary Values in the order shown below.

Card Sort #1:

Recognition

Autonomy

Intellectual Challenge

Variety

Helping Others

Card Sort #2:

Intellectual Challenge

Helping Others

Recognition

Autonomy

Variety

From these two lists, we see that Recognition came before Autonomy and Variety both times. We also see that Intellectual Challenge came before Helping Others and Variety both times. So either Recognition or Intellectual Challenge would be your top value, with the other coming in second. Autonomy, Helping Others, and Variety would follow in any order, as long as Autonomy precedes Variety. Variety would likely come in last, as it was ranked four and five in the card sorts. Now try this with your own Primary Values. Rank them below according to their priority. Limit your list to the top five.

Top Five Values

_____

_____

_____

_____

_____

EXERCISE #6. PERSONALIZING YOUR VALUES

Now that you have a list of your Top Values, you need to personalize them. It's not enough to have a list of words representing abstract concepts. You need to know what these concepts mean for you, and how you want them manifested in your work. Look at your number one Top Value. What does it mean to you to want that? What are some examples of times in the past when you've had that? And what are some examples of times when it was absent, compromised, or restricted? What does your number one Top Value look like in an ideal job setting? If you could create it any way you want, how would you create it? Be specific. Begin to shape your personalized version of that value.

_____

_____

_____

Do the same for your other top values:

_____

_____

_____

_____

_____

_____

_____

_____

_____

_____

_____

_____

_____

_____

_____

_____

_____

_____

As you are thinking about personalizing your values, it is useful to distinguish between *means values* and *end values*. A means value is important to you because it helps you achieve something even more important. That "something" is an end value, which is really an intrinsic, ongoing experience you want to have because it's part of your identity. So how do you determine which is which? When you consider a value you find important, reflect on the answer to this statement: "*I want this value so that* ...." If you can come up with an answer, then it's a means value. If you can't come up with an answer, other than that you just really want to experience that value in your life on an ongoing basis, it's an end value. It's your bottom line.

Example: Let's say you selected Creative Expression as one of your Top Values. Ask yourself: "I want Creative Expression so that..." If your answer is, "*That's the bottom line; I just really want to express myself,*" then it's an end value. But if you say, "*I want to create something because I want to help people...*or *achieve recognition...or be admired*", or, "*Because when I express myself, I feel effective,*" then it's a means value. For you, Creative Expression is a means to an even greater end.

EXERCISE #7. DISTINGUISHING MEANS VALUES FROM END VALUES

Now it's your turn. For each of your Top Values, ask yourself why the particular value is important to you. Don't stop until you drill down to the essential underlying experience you want to have. When you start repeating yourself and there is no other answer, then you've hit the end value.

Top Value #1: _____ [Means/End] [Circle one]

I want this so that _____

My end value is: _____

Top Value #2: _____ [Means/End] [Circle one]

I want this so that_____

My end value is: _____

Top Value #3: _____ [Means/End] [Circle one]

I want this so that_____

My end value is: _____

Top Value #4: _____ [Means/End] [Circle one]

I want this so that_____

My end value is: _____

Top Value #5: _____ [Means/End] [Circle one]

I want this so that_____

My end value is: _____

So far, you have done a lot of exercises intended to uncover and clarify what is most important to you in a job. You have identified your primary and secondary worldview values systems; identified your primary and secondary career anchors; and identified, classified, prioritized, and personalized your top values through the values card sort. You have even distinguished between your means values and end values.

How do you make sense of all this information? The most important thing to look for is repetition. I have been asking you about your values in several different ways. The reason it is so important to do all these exercises is because when you gather a lot of data about your values, using different techniques, and some common themes emerge, that gives you a very high confidence level that you've identified your core values. The more central a value is to your career identity, the more often it will show up. Your most fundamental, deeply held values will surface no matter how the question is asked or what kind of exercise you do. They are like grass growing through the sidewalk—they pop up through all the cracks.

So take a look back over your answers to the exercises in this chapter. What do you notice? Are there pervasive themes? Which values consistently rise to the top?

You should now have a pretty clear idea of your values—the most crucial element of your career identity. This awareness alone puts you considerably ahead of where you were before you did the exercises in this chapter. Now, you are going to build on this foundation by discovering the next element of your career identity—your psychological needs—which is the subject of Chapter 7.

Does Your Job Fit Your Psychological Needs?

In this chapter, I talk about your psychological needs, and why you won't find true job satisfaction unless those needs are met. Psychological needs do not operate on a continuum like values. Whereas values operate like a dimmer switch, psychological needs operate like an on-off switch. A need is either met or not. If you have a psychological need that is not being met, it can draw your attention, even at the expense of your values, until it is met. If you're thinking about changing jobs or careers, and you have a need that's very important to you—and it's being met in your current job—you may fail to consider it. You may even overlook this need because it's being met, and it's not on your radar screen.

Do you ever feel frustrated when working or when you think about your job? If you answered yes, there is a good chance that one or more of your psychological needs is not getting met. On the other hand, when a need is being met, the only thing you will feel is the absence of frustration. In other words, there is no positive emotion to tell you that a particular need is being met. Needs that are being met are often "invisible"; off the radar screen. So if you never experience frustration at work, then your job likely fulfills most or all of your psychological needs.

Consider the case of Lisa, a district attorney. She initially found the job challenging but eventually burned out and got bored. So she went to work for the Attorney General's office in the appellate division and found the work stimulating and challenging. To her surprise, however, she also found it very quiet and isolating. She didn't realize how much she would miss the camaraderie of the people she worked with.

When evaluating her job as a DA, she failed to consider her need for connection, because it was being met at the time. So it didn't occur to her to make sure she would get that need met in the Attorney General's office.

This is an all too common scenario. But it doesn't have to be your fate, if you take the time to discover your own psychological needs. In this chapter, I will present you with a simple exercise to identify and prioritize your psychological needs. You will then have clarified the second most important element of your career identity.

Basic Psychological Needs

All human beings have certain basic psychological needs, although in varying degrees. Here are some of the most common needs that have been identified by psychological research. Needs can be interpersonal or intrapersonal. Interpersonal needs occur with reference to other people, while intrapersonal needs are self-focused.

Let's begin with a look at a few of the main interpersonal needs:

The need for affiliation or inclusion. Whether we get that need met by actively including others or by passively being included, the subjective feeling is the same. No one likes feeling "left out". But some of us have a greater need than others to feel like we're part of a group or organization, or to feel like we belong among others who we perceive as being like us.

The need for power or control. Again, you can achieve that feeling by controlling others or by submitting to the structure that others provide. In either case you may experience a sense of security, either because you're the one in control or because someone else has provided structure for you. The subjective experience is that you don't feel out of control and chaotic. Lawyers, more than most other people, have a strong need for control. They don't like to be told what to do by others.

The need for openness. When a person has a high need for openness, they seek out connections with others, and more readily disclose private feelings to others in order to deepen the relationship. Everyone needs intimacy to some degree in their personal relationships, but some people also need intimacy in their work.

Other psychological needs include approval, security, effectiveness, closure, affection, precision, continuity, and predictability. Needs are held internally in some sort of rough hierarchy. Some are more important to you than others.

Case study #1. *Let's take the case of David, a young associate who works for just one other lawyer in the firm. David has a high need for approval, but his boss is one of those tough-minded lawyers who never say, "Thank you" or, "Great job." The only way David knows he has done well is when his boss doesn't criticize him. David has a really hard time working for this person and feels frustrated much of the time. Once he is conscious of his need for approval—and that it's not being met—he has several possible choices. David could look for an exit strategy—either from the firm, department, or reporting arrangement—to find more compatible work. Or, he could decide to develop a strategy to better manage his response when this need is not met.*

Case study #2. *One of the more common psychological needs in lawyers is the need for effectiveness. Take the example of Nancy, a tax lawyer with a strong need to feel authoritative and effective. Her tax expertise gave her that feeling and fulfilled that need. But she was ready to throw out her entire body of expertise, leave the law, and go into a new field—all because she didn't like the environment she was practicing in. She was so unhappy that she was ready to throw in the towel. But because her need for effectiveness was getting met, it was off her radar screen. All she could think about was what she disliked about her job and firm.*

Case study #3. *One of the needs that lawyers frequently overlook is the need for intimacy or connection. We all have some need for intimacy, but lawyers don't like to talk about it, and often don't even realize that they have some of this need. Lawyers in general tend to be low in this need, but if you have a need for connection at work that is going unmet, you are going to be very frustrated. Consider the case of Eric, a lawyer who went from working as a transactional lawyer in finance in a large firm to a non-law job where he was running a branch of a company doing legal and business research. Because his job required him to do research on his computer, he would sit alone at home, working in front of his computer all day long. At first he thought this would be a real benefit, but after awhile it began to drive him crazy. He realized he had miscalculated, underestimating his needs for intimacy, connection, and inclusion.*

EXERCISE #1. IDENTIFYING AND PRIORITIZING YOUR PSYCHOLOGICAL NEEDS

You can determine your own needs hierarchy. Remember that repetition is the way to confirm the importance of any given element of your identity. Rank the following psychological needs in the order of their importance to you. As with the previous ranking exercise for values, this is an emotional process; don't try to subject your needs to logic. Your strongest psychological needs will eventually rise to the surface.

_____Inclusion

_____Control

_____Openness

_____Approval

_____Security

_____Effectiveness

_____Closure

_____Affection

_____Intimacy

_____Connection

_____Precision

_____Continuity

_____Predictability

After at least two weeks, repeat this exercise without referring to the first results.

_____Inclusion

_____Control

_____Openness

_____Approval

_____Security

_____Effectiveness

_____Closure

_____Affection

_____Intimacy

_____Connection

_____Precision

_____Continuity

_____Predictability

Compare the results of both exercises. Focus on the needs at the top and bottom of your lists. Are they similar? Looking at the order of your needs on both lists, prioritize each need from top to bottom. Example: Let's say that your two ranking exercises yielded the following needs in the order shown below.

Ranking #1:		Ranking #2:	
_3_	Inclusion	_7_	Inclusion
_5_	Control	_8_	Control
_8_	Openness	_3_	Openness
_6_	Approval	_6_	Approval
_11_	Security	_12_	Security
_2_	Effectiveness	_2_	Effectiveness
_9_	Closure	_10_	Closure
_7_	Affection	_5_	Affection
_4_	Intimacy	_4_	Intimacy
_1_	Connection	_1_	Connection
_10_	Precision	_9_	Precision
_12_	Continuity	_11_	Continuity
_13_	Predictability	_13_	Predictability

One way to prioritize the 13 needs, based on the above two rankings, is the following:

1. Connection—1 in both rankings
2. Effectiveness—2 in both rankings
3. Openness—8 in 1st ranking; 3 in 2nd ranking
4. Intimacy—4 in both rankings
5. Affection—7 in 1st ranking; 5 in 2nd ranking
6. Approval—6 in both rankings
7. Inclusion—3 in 1st ranking; 7 in 2nd ranking
8. Control—5 in 1st ranking; 8 in 2nd ranking
9. Precision—10 in 1st ranking; 9 in 2nd ranking
10. Closure—9 in 1st ranking; 10 in 2nd ranking
11. Continuity—12 in 1st ranking; 11 in 2nd ranking
12. Security—11 in 1st ranking; 12 in 2nd ranking
13. Predictability—13 in both rankings

As you can see, numbers 1, 2, 4, 6, and 13 were ranked the same in both rankings of our example. Numbers 9 and 10 just swapped spots, as did 11 and 12.

Numbers 3, 5, 7, and 8 moved around more between the rankings. There is no pattern, except that inclusion was ranked before control in both rankings. So you could use your judgment as to how you choose to rank these four needs. In the above example, I simply used the 2nd ranking to prioritize the needs.

Now try this with your own psychological needs. Prioritize them in order of importance to you.

1. _____
2. _____
3. _____
4. _____
5. _____
6. _____
7. _____
8. _____
9. _____
10. _____
11. _____
12. _____
13. _____

You now have the second most important element of your career identity.

EXERCISE #2. ASSESSING NEEDS FULFILLMENT

It's just as important to identify the needs that are being met as it is to identify the ones that are not being met. In this exercise, consider whether your needs are getting met in your current job. If you are not employed now, use your most recent work experience. Look at your list of prioritized psychological needs. Which ones are/were met? Which ones are/were not? List them below.

Needs	Fulfilled Needs	Unfulfilled Needs
Inclusion	_____	_____
Control	_____	_____
Openness	_____	_____

Approval	_____	_____
Security	_____	_____
Effectiveness	_____	_____
Closure	_____	_____
Affection	_____	_____
Intimacy	_____	_____
Connection	_____	_____
Precision	_____	_____
Continuity	_____	_____
Predictability	_____	_____

In looking at your two lists, what do you notice? Are more of your needs fulfilled or unfulfilled? Is there anything surprising about your lists? Are there needs that are currently getting met that you weren't even aware of? If so, it will be very important for you to keep these in mind if you decide to change jobs or careers.

Our Needs vs. Our Values

What is the difference between needs and values?

Values operate along a continuum. With values, it's possible to think of situations in which more and more and more of a particular value will make you happier and happier. Conversely, less and less of that value would make you increasingly disappointed or angry. It's possible to get your values met partway along a continuum.

With needs, however, you want a certain amount of it, and anything less is not satisfactory.

Example: when most people think about their need for security, they're thinking about a certain level of reassurance they want. If they don't get that level of reassurance, then it doesn't really matter if they still have a little reassurance. They will still experience frustration. Likewise, when you probe most people for what they mean by their need for control, they have a certain experience in mind. If they don't achieve that full experience, a partial fulfillment of that need just isn't satisfying. Needs trump values temporarily until they're met, but there is unlikely to be a permanent conflict between your needs and your values.

If you have a need that is unmet, you're going to experience significant frustration and even desperation.

You probably won't tolerate that situation for long. Once the need is met, it disappears from your radar screen. The distinction between values and needs is not always so clear-cut. Take security, for example. It is one of the career anchors, and it's also one of the values on the card sort. Yet many also consider it a compelling psychological need.

What if some of my needs appear to conflict? Lawyers often ask questions about the logical inconsistencies either within a category—like two seemingly conflicting needs—or between categories. "How can I need both intimacy and autonomy?" they ask. Or, "How can I be both urgent and cautious?" The answer is that your identity is based on emotion, not on logic. Remarkably, the human mind subconsciously harmonizes seemingly inconsistent elements of your identity. Only if you impose a rule of logic do they appear inconsistent.

You should now have a clear idea of your most basic psychological needs and their order of priority—which is the second most important element of your career identity, and something that most people never discover about themselves. Let's proceed to the next element: your communication style.

CHAPTER 8

Does Your Job Fit Your Communication Style?

To find true career satisfaction, you must do more than simply avoid an unpleasant work environment. You need to understand how your personal communication style fits key aspects of your job. In this chapter, I will describe the four dimensions of communication style. A simple exercise will help determine the fit between your job and your overall communication style, and also between your job and each of the four dimensions of your style.

In the previous chapters, you identified your values and psychological needs. Now we turn to the next most important element of career satisfaction—your communication style. In this chapter, I will describe the basic dimensions of communication style so that you can identify your own style.

Do you sometimes feel like a fish out of water at work?
Do you ever feel confused or alienated?
Do you like your work, but feel that your coworkers are just not "your type"?
Or, do you like the people but feel disconnected from the type of work you do,
    like something is just not quite right even though it seems like a
    good job?

If you answered yes to any of these questions, it is likely that your job does not fit with your overall communication style or with one or more elements of your style. On the other hand, if your preferred communication style fits the prevailing style of others in your workplace, you probably experience a sense of camaraderie. And if your overall style fits the work you do, you probably feel a sense of congruence with your job.

For example, Anna was a lawyer with a communication style characterized by warmth and nurturing. She initially got a job at a law firm with an impersonal, austere, "eat-what-you-kill" atmosphere. Not surprisingly, she was very unhappy. For the most part, Anna liked being a lawyer, but she was completely miserable in her work environment. Anna almost made the mistake of changing professions altogether. But then she found a job at a firm with an open, informal, friendly culture. Anna not only enjoyed her colleagues and work environment at the new firm, but she found that she took more satisfaction in practicing law.

Communication Style: the Basics

Everyone develops patterns in the way they interact with people, deal with data, make decisions, schedule events, and a range of other behaviors. Put simply, *your communication style is your patterned, habitual behavior or way of dealing with people, data, decisions, and events.* The system of communication style described in this chapter is based on the work of psychoanalyst Carl Jung and his Theory of Psychological Types. The personality types he identified can be measured by several different tools, but the most well-known and widely used is the Myers-Briggs Type Indicator (MBTI).

The MBTI is a formal professional tool that can be administered only by someone specifically trained and certified to do so. The many unofficial free tests on the Internet are not scientifically validated and should not be relied on. Many career counselors and coaches, placement officials, guidance counselors, therapists, and others have been trained and certified in the official MBTI instrument. A couple of books that do a good job of authoritatively discussing personality types (using the MBTI model) are *Type Talk at Work* (Kroeger, Thuesen) and *Do What You Are* (Tieger, Barron-Tieger).

The MBTI measures your preferences along four dimensions:

- E/I (Extraversion vs. Introversion)
- S/N (Sensing vs. Intuition)
- T/F (Thinking vs. Feeling)
- J/P (Judging vs. Perceiving)

Each of us has an independent preference on each of these four dimensions. Our preferences tend to be stable, long term, and pervasive. Each of the different preferences is legitimate, and no single preference is better or worse than any other. Knowing your preference on each of these dimensions (i.e., are you an ENFJ, an ISTJ, etc.?) provides important information about the types of people you will enjoy working with, the kinds of tasks you're likely to enjoy, the variety of information you'll prefer dealing with, and the kinds of work experiences that are likely to give you satisfaction.

Let's look at each of the dimensions separately.

Extraversion vs. Introversion (E/I). This first dimension measures where you prefer to focus your energy:

Extraverts pay more attention to the world outside their psyche. If you are an extravert, you may enjoy thinking out loud just to clarify your thoughts. You may like variety and prefer speaking to writing. Opportunities to be around people will be important.

Introverts pay more attention to their inner world of thoughts, feelings, and sense impressions. If you are an introvert, you may prefer focusing on one issue at a time and thinking it through before discussing it. You probably enjoy periodic opportunities for solitude and enjoy writing.

Extraverts are more likely to be gregarious, to enjoy client contact, and to prefer discussing a legal matter more than writing about it. They may positively enjoy the rainmaking process, are more likely to join clubs and bar associations, and will prefer breadth and variety in their work. *Introverts*, on the other hand, tend to be more reserved, prefer working alone or in one-on-one relationships, and enjoy analyzing and writing about a legal issue. Their thinking is usually done silently. They tend to prefer concentrating on a topic in depth, thinking it through and reflecting on it. The same events that an Extravert would find exciting and energizing—parties, crowds, networking events—may be experienced by an Introvert as over-stimulating, "too much," or simply not enjoyable.

In the United States, Extraverts constitute a clear majority. In contrast, a slight majority of lawyers prefer Introversion. Although more Introverts are attracted to law, both male and female Extravert lawyers have reported slightly higher job satisfaction than their Introverted counterparts. One possible explanation might be that Introverted lawyers may be weary from too much client contact or work in an office setting that is mismatched to their communication preference. This particular aspect of your communication style can influence your comfort level in the office environment. Strong Introverts can feel really out of place in a boisterous, high-energy office. While less common, the opposite can be true for Extraverts in a quiet, low-energy office.

Case study #1. *Consider the case of Karen, who was extremely Introverted. Before becoming a lawyer, she worked as a computer programmer. Karen had a very low tolerance for social interaction and was quite happy working alone. Her idea of a good day was to sit in front of the computer all day without much people contact. Once she got a job as a litigator in a traditional law firm and*

*realized how much interaction with people it entailed, she didn't want to stay
in the law. She had an overwhelming need for solitude, which was at odds with
the demands of her job to interact with coworkers, clients, and opposing counsel.
When she first came to career counseling, Karen didn't even mention this as
the cause of her dissatisfaction. To Karen, her need for quiet and solo work was
just one of her many attributes. She thought she was just not cut out to practice
law. If she hadn't explored other practice areas and work environments, she
might have left the law altogether. Instead, she began to look into the possibility
of doing appellate work for the government, which involved a lot more time
analyzing issues and less time interacting with others.*

Case study #2. *On the other end of the Extraversion/Introversion dimension,
consider Brian, a lawyer with a very clear Extraversion preference who worked
as a staff lawyer in a relatively quiet local government office full of Introverts
working with their doors closed most of the time. Brian would walk the halls
every day, looking for willing participants to discuss cases, chat about personal
lives, and listen to his jokes and stories. Friends would describe him as an
"exuberant personality", the life of all the office parties, and the center of lively
lunchroom banter. While his coworkers liked Brian, and appreciated his good
humor and upbeat personality, they often did not share his desire to sit around
and have lengthy conversations. Brian felt like he couldn't really be himself
at work, and it was only in his personal life that he found an outlet for his
social nature. He might have found a better fit in an office setting with other
Extraverts.*

Sensing vs. Intuition (S/N). This second dimension measures how and what
type of information you gather:

Sensors prefer to gather their information from the observable world
around them—things that can be seen, heard, touched, and verified by
experience. If this is your preferred way of gathering information, you're
probably realistic, practical, and comfortable with facts and some degree
of detail.

Intuitives prefer to gather their information from hunches, and by
paying attention to concepts and abstractions. They more often pay attention to the meaning *behind* the data than to the data itself. If this is your
preferred way of gathering information, you probably enjoy speculating
about what *could* be more than looking at what is. You may consider yourself a "big picture" person and may enjoy ingenuity and creativity, playing
with language, and constructing theories.

Sensors are more comfortable with concrete, specific, factual data; the kinds of information you get from your five senses. They usually prefer low ambiguity, well-defined tasks, and a no-nonsense approach to work. They are focused on the present, seek practical and tangible results, and are more interested in analyzing data than abstractions. Regulatory and code-based practice areas appeal to them. *Intuitives* are more comfortable with abstract, impressionistic, or theoretical information. They tend to be more focused on the future. What may appeal more to them are practice areas involving conceptual or philosophical issues such as constitutional law or litigation in which they can create new legal theories.

A majority of men and women in the United States prefer Sensing to Intuition, but there are slightly more Intuitives in the lawyer population.

Typical tasks in the early years of law practice draw more on Sensing than Intuiting. This can be very frustrating for strong Intuitives, leaving some of them to draw the conclusion—prematurely and perhaps mistakenly—that they would be better off in a different profession.

Case study #3. *Take the case of Chris, a young associate in a large law firm. Chris was assigned typical young lawyer projects: researching individual and discrete points of law; drafting and reviewing documents; combing through transcripts of depositions and answers to interrogatories, etc.—all without usually having any context of the case or contact with the client. Even though he liked his coworkers, Chris was completely miserable, stuck in the law library, thinking that he had made a horrible mistake in his career choice. But he opened up to other more senior associates and a few junior partners, who shared that they, too, had had similar experiences as a junior associate. Chris decided to stay in the law, at least for a little while longer. As he advanced in his career, he was given more and more responsibility. He got to consult with more senior lawyers on the larger "big picture" issues of cases, and eventually got to handle some of his own cases through from start to finish. This made all the difference, allowing Chris to more fully use his preference for Intuition.*

Lawyers whose job doesn't fit their Sensing preference have many options to remedy their dissatisfaction, because so many jobs—inside and out of the law—require a high degree of attention to facts and details.

Case study #4. *Tom, Diane, and Christine all began their legal careers in the same law firm, working on high-profile business litigation cases. They each experienced a similar disconnect with their work, feeling impatient with all the discussions about case strategies and litigation theories. They didn't get* *why anyone would want to spend time talking about esoteric points of the law when, in their view, the case would be won or lost on the facts. Tom, Diane, and Christine took different paths from there, each according to his or her career identity. Tom decided to join a firm with a practice group specializing in compliance advice to financial institutions. He felt very comfortable with the bright lines of the regulations that governed this practice area. Diane decided to open her own estate planning practice, and reveled in all the practical business aspects of running a law firm. Christine took yet another course, deciding to leave the law and work in investment banking, with its emphasis on statistical analysis and number-crunching.*

Thinking vs. Feeling (T/F). This third dimension identifies how you make decisions or draw conclusions about data:

> **Thinkers** rely on logical and objective analysis to reach a conclusion. Although they may have strong feelings or strong preferences about the thing to be decided, they usually make a conscious attempt to put those feelings aside and not allow them to influence their thinking.
> **Feelers** use a more personal, subjective strategy to reach a conclusion, and consider their own personal values when making a decision. They typically ask themselves values-based questions such as, "Do I like X?" or "Do I want X?" or "How would X affect others?"

Thinkers tend to be critical and receive criticism from others as mere data, while Feelers allow the emotions in along with the data. Thus, Feelers may get their feelings bruised more easily. Because of this, *Feelers* also pay more attention to maintenance behaviors—harmonizing, avoiding conflict, paying compliments, etc. Thinkers are attracted to the realm of the mind. Ask a Thinker, "Why did you go into law?", and you'll likely hear the words "intellectual challenge" as the answer. Ask a Feeler the same question and you may hear answers such as "to help people" or "to promote social justice." The Thinker versus Feeler dimension holds special significance for the legal profession. This preference is gender-sensitive in the general population but not in law. A majority of men in the United States prefer the Thinking style, while a majority of all women prefer the Feeling style.

The practice of law attracts far more Thinkers than Feelers relative to the proportions in the general population. In fact, the vast majority of both male and female lawyers prefer the Thinking style, and there are even some law firms in which virtually all males are Thinkers. The Thinking preference is one of the hallmarks of the legal profession.

Because the law places such an emphasis on logic, intellectual reasoning, conflict, adversarial thinking, and being able to argue any side of a matter, there is a very strong bias in favor of the Thinker style and against the Feeler style. Perhaps the most confused lawyers are those who find themselves attracted to both styles to a limited extent. If you fall into this category, then both of these decisional styles will appeal to you, and you may already have had the experience of being attracted to the intellectual challenge offered by law practice while at the same time being put off by the combative nature of your work.

Case study #5. *Steve was a plaintiff's lawyer. He was decidedly a Feeler, and Feelers tend to dislike conflict. Every time he had to go to court or argue with opposing counsel, it upset him. Eventually, he came to feel kind of dead inside whenever he had to deal with conflict, and he was ambivalent about continuing to practice law. But while Steve found his work incredibly frustrating at times, he didn't want to give it up. His sense of purpose in advocating for "the little guy", and the values he held that were validated in his work, outweighed even his discomfort with the adversarial nature of his job. After assessing his career identity, Steve came to realize that he was willing to tolerate conflict now and then in order to fulfill his sense of mission, which was a daily experience for him. Having looked at his situation with fresh eyes, Steve was willing to accept this tradeoff.*

Just because this one aspect of your communication style (Thinking vs. Feeling) doesn't fit your job is not in itself enough reason to give up the practice of law. On the other hand, even if there are many other sources of gratification for you in the law, if you are a strong Feeler, you will likely often feel as though you are swimming against the current while practicing law. Your key task here is to find a job that is congruent with your Feeler preference at least a majority of the time.

Case study #6. *Charles had a strong Feeler preference—unusually strong for a lawyer. He wore his heart on his sleeve, his demeanor was totally open, and his emotions were completely available. Charles worked in a very old-school, buttoned-up, traditional business practice that was a mismatch for him on many levels, especially with his communication style. But he didn't see it. He was blind to his situation but really wanted to make the law work for him. Charles eventually realized that he would never be happy in a job that required him to repress his empathetic, nurturing Feeler qualities. Charles ended up leaving private practice and went to work for a nonprofit—a job that allowed* *expression of his Feeler preference, and provided a much better fit for all of his career identity.*

Judging vs. Perceiving (J/P). The fourth dimension measures your style in dealing with tasks and people:

> **Judgers** approach the world in a planned, orderly, and decisive way. If this sounds like you, you probably often like to "cut to the chase" and feel more comfortable when your week is carefully planned. You know where your files are and you make to-do lists and check things off.
>
> **Perceivers** approach the world in an open, spontaneous, and flexible manner. If this sounds more like you, you probably like to "keep your options open" and may resist making decisions until the last possible moment. You may be more comfortable working at a desk where everything you might have to work on is laid out within easy reach.

Judgers tend to do only one thing at a time; they complete assignments in an orderly and timely manner to avoid the last-minute rush; they keep small manageable lists of things to do, methodically checking off completed items; they make decisions at the earliest possible point, without waiting for all information; they keep a neat desk; and they plan for all possible contingencies in advance. *Perceivers* juggle many tasks, often doing more than one at a time; they "play it by ear"; they make many lengthy lists (and sometimes lose them); they put off decisions to gather more complete information; they maintain piles in their office, any one of which can be worked on spontaneously; they avoid committing themselves to plans until the last minute; and they may even enjoy surprises.

A majority of lawyers prefer Judging, about 10 percent more than the general public. It makes sense that a profession that has many deadlines and requires a great deal of organizational skills from its practitioners would attract more people with preferences for using these kinds of skills.

Case study #7. *As a strong Perceiver, Henry found himself at odds with the communication style of his coworkers and the demands of his practice. Henry was a talented litigator and case strategist, and also very gifted at interpersonal communication. However, he was always getting into trouble by misplacing files, underestimating the time required for a task, and missing deadlines. And the strict court procedures and protocol were anathema to Henry, who wished everyone could simply "go with the flow" more. His relaxed nature sometimes drove his coworkers crazy, and they were often at odds in their preferences for* *how to run a practice. Although a good administrative support system in the office saved Henry from making any major mistakes, he always felt like his hands were a bit tied. Henry eventually transitioned to mediation, where he excelled at the more informal setting and relations between the parties, and he didn't have to comply with as many deadlines, rules, and paper burdens.*

Case study #8. *Julia, an associate, abhorred having to bill hours and account for her time in six-minute increments. Not many lawyers love billable hours, but Julia disliked them more intensely than most. With her Perceiving preference, what Julia wanted most was to be able to lose herself in a project for hours at a time without interruption. She wanted to spend whatever time she felt was necessary to do the work adequately, without regard to what she viewed as restrictive requirements for efficiency. This mismatch between her style and the demands of private practice led Julia to explore other careers. Drawn to teaching, she tested the waters by becoming an instructor at a paralegal college. She eventually was able to secure a position as a law professor, first as an adjunct and later as full-time faculty. Academia proved to be the perfect fit, where she could spend hours in research, contemplative thought, and curriculum planning.*

EXERCISE #1. ASSESSING FULFILLMENT OF YOUR COMMUNICATION STYLE

In this exercise, reflect on how well your job fits your overall communication style and your individual preferences. Think in terms of the following categories: *Very Good Fit; Good Fit; Somewhat Good Fit; Somewhat Bad Fit; Bad Fit; Very Bad Fit*. On each continuum, mark an "X" on the spot that represents your best estimate of the fit between your job and your preference in that dimension, or between your job and your overall style. If you are not currently working, think about your most recent work experience as you consider your communication style.

Extraversion vs. Introversion

Sensing vs. Intuition

Thinking vs. Feeling

|____|____|____|____|____|____|

Judging vs. Perceiving

|____|____|____|____|____|____|

Your Overall Communication Style

|____|____|____|____|____|____|

Communication Style and Practice Area

Your choice of practice area may be influenced by your communication style.

- On the **Extraversion vs. Introversion** dimension, for instance, three legal specialties have been found to attract significantly more Extraverts: torts and insurance, general civil litigation, and labor law. If you have a strong preference for Extraversion yourself, and one or more of these practice areas appeals to you, you might consider exploring these fields.
- The **Sensing vs. Intuition** dimension is highly correlated with choice of practice area. More Intuitives than Sensors are drawn to law in general. However, if you have a clear preference for Sensing, you might consider developing an expertise in a particular substantive area with low ambiguity. Regulatory and code-based practice areas such as tax, securities, and many administrative law specialties will feel much more natural to the strong Sensor. Three legal specialty areas have been found to attract more than their fair share of Sensors: securities law, real estate, and tax/trusts/estates as well as general practice. Likewise, three practice areas have been found to attract a disproportionate number of Intuitives: criminal law, labor law, and general civil litigation. If you are comfortable with both Sensing and Intuition, most areas of the law will fit. If you are a strong Intuitive, choose a practice area that will expose you to conceptual issues or one in which gray areas abound.
- On the **Thinking vs. Feeling** dimension, two legal specialties have been found to attract greater proportions of Feeler women: labor law and litigation. Three legal specialties have been found to attract greater proportions of Feeler men: general practice, criminal law, and domestic relations. For all Feelers, litigation can be a two-edged sword. Many Feelers are attracted to the field because it holds the promise of effecting social change (a value for many Feelers); on the other hand, it represents an area of the law with perhaps the greatest ongoing interpersonal

conflict (a situation that most Feelers disdain). Lawyers with a Thinker preference—male and female alike—have found job satisfaction in nearly every legal specialty imaginable.

- On the **Judging vs. Perceiving** dimension, labor lawyers have reported more Perceivers than any other area. Other areas with somewhat more Perceivers than Judgers include criminal law, general practice, and litigation. As with the Feeling realm, Perceivers in litigation are using a two-edged sword. The "play it by ear" style of the Perceiver can cope well with and enjoys a fast-breaking change in circumstances common to litigation. On the flip side, many Perceivers also tend to be a bit disorganized, and the consequences of this style in litigation can be more harsh and immediate than perhaps any other legal specialty.

Your Communication Style and Work Setting

Your choice of work setting may be influenced by your preference on the Extraversion versus Introversion dimension. As mentioned earlier, Introverts might feel out of place in a high-energy office, and Extraverts may feel like fish out of water in a quiet work environment. For example, a majority of lawyers working in the government have been found to prefer Introversion. If you are thinking about accepting a particular job offer, spend some time in the office of your potential employer and pay attention to the energy.

Your choice of a work setting also may be influenced by your preferences on the Sensing versus Intuition dimension. Two settings in particular have attracted a disproportionate number of Intuitives: judicial clerkships and legal aid and public defender offices. This makes sense, as most clerkships offer the promise of dealing with legal jurisprudence, the kinds of conceptual and philosophical issues that Intuitives find appealing. Sensors prefer more practical objectives and thus are more likely to look for a first job that allows them to roll their sleeves up and get to work as a lawyer, such as a position at a traditional law firm.

Thinker lawyers have reported only a slightly higher level of job satisfaction than Feeler lawyers. Despite the minority status of Feelers in the profession, many of them have found satisfaction in what is clearly a Thinker profession, possibly by choosing work environments wisely. As one example, more lawyers working for legal aid or public defender offices were Feelers than compared with all lawyers as a whole.

Not only are Judgers more prevalent in the legal profession, but they have reported greater job satisfaction as well. The only work setting to which significantly more Perceivers are attracted is legal aid and public defender offices. If this type of work appeals to you, you may find that your Perceiving preference fits right in. The best advice for lawyers with strong Perceiver preferences is to surround themselves with a support staff that has strong Judging preferences, and to count on them to add structure that you yourself may not provide. This strategy can enable even the strongest Perceiver to find satisfaction in the law.

As you consider the fit between your own communication style and various practice areas and work settings, keep in mind that it is possible for lawyers with every combination of preferences to find job satisfaction. There is no combination of the four preferences that has reported more dissatisfied lawyers than satisfied lawyers.

Although your communication style is an important element of your career identity, this one element alone does not determine your job or career satisfaction. We have already explored your values and psychological needs, which heavily influence career satisfaction. In the next chapter, we will explore the next element of your career identity—your motivated skills.

CHAPTER 9

Does Your Job Fit Your Motivated Skills?

In the world of career counseling, there is a school of thought that one's aptitudes and skills—that is, behaviors that a person is good at, whether innate or learned—are a good measure of what a person would like to do for a job. The consensus is that if you're good at something, you will like doing it. This chapter helps explain why the area of "skills" poses a special trap for lawyers. In the pages ahead, you will have an opportunity to identify and prioritize your motivated skills, and to assess how well your work fulfills these skills.

You have now identified three of the most important elements of your career identity—your values, your psychological needs, and your communication style. In this chapter, we explore the next element—your Motivated Skills.

Do you ever feel like your work is tedious?

Does your job feel like drudgery?

Do you ever feel a sense of emptiness at work, like something is missing but you just can't put your finger on it?

Is there some special skill or talent that you would love to get paid for but aren't using in your job?

If you can identify with any of these experiences, it is likely that either your job requires you to use skills you don't enjoy using, or you don't get to use skills in your job that you do enjoy using. On the other hand, if your job allows you to use those skills that you both like and perform well, and you identify with those skills, you probably experience a feeling of effectiveness.

I have seen many clients, however, who became extremely good at something but didn't enjoy doing it. For example, Cheryl was asked by a senior lawyer in her firm to research the nuances of the latest developments in residential foreclosures. Before she knew it, she was the designated expert in her firm on this topic, and all the new foreclosure matters that came through the door landed on her desk, even though she actually detested handling these types of cases. Cheryl got pigeonholed into a specialty she couldn't stand, all because she complied with another lawyer's request for help and performed well.

I myself am another example of this. I was really good at math in school, receiving some of the highest scores in certain classes. I also scored very well in the math section of the SAT test. But I found math extremely tedious and would never want a career in which I had to use that skill. You can probably think of several things you are good at that you wouldn't want to do for a living.

Motivated Skills Defined

In addition to being good at something, you also must enjoy doing it if you want to achieve long-term career satisfaction. In other words, you must be *motivated* to use that skill. Merely being good at something is not enough to sustain you in the law and, by itself, is not a good predictor of whether you will like a particular job. *You need to be good at it and enjoy using it—enjoy it to the extent that it's part of your identity.* Among lawyers, the most common scenario is the person who has a particular skill but has never examined whether he or she likes using it or not.

> *Having to do something you are good at but don't enjoy produces tedium. On the other hand, if you have a skill that you don't get to use, it produces a feeling of emptiness or something missing—it's like a piece of you is unfulfilled.*

Case study #1. *Tim is a good example of both of these situations. Tim worked at a high-powered law firm doing complex corporate and real estate transactions. He had great business sense and was financially savvy. He excelled at both the strategic and technical aspects of the deals. The problem was that Tim didn't enjoy using these skills, so the work felt like drudgery to him despite being very good at it. In addition, Tim had strong interpersonal skills that he enjoyed using but didn't get to employ to their fullest extent in his current job. After realizing that he was not using his motivated skills, Tim left his law firm job and went to work in fundraising and development at a law school. His new job did not require him to use skills he found tedious, and allowed him full expression of the skills he did enjoy using.*

The Trap for Lawyers

The motivated skills element poses a special trap for lawyers.

I always begin an initial counseling session with a new client by asking the question, *"What made you decide to be a lawyer?"* Some people say things like, *"I didn't decide. It just happened."* Or, *"I decided against other careers, and the next thing I knew, I was in law school."* Well, that's just not true. You don't get into law school by accident. You have to apply. You have to fill out numerous forms. But what these lawyers are saying is that they applied to law school because they didn't know what else to do. It was the default choice, but a choice nonetheless. When I press these clients further, they often say something like this: *"Well, when I was a kid, I was really good at arguing."* Or, *"When I was in high school, I was really good at debating."* Or they say that they were very good at writing or analyzing or persuading. It's a common refrain among lawyers. You've probably heard someone (perhaps even you) say something similar.

After making these statements, the clients often just stop, as if inviting the listener to make the assumption—the logical jump—as they did, that because they were good at a particular skill that lawyers use, that they should be a lawyer. I refuse to take that intuitive leap. Instead, I question them further: *"Well, did you enjoy debating?"* Interestingly, a number of them say, *"Well, no, not really. I was really good at it, but in hindsight, I don't know if I wanted to build a life on that. It's just something I was good at; it wasn't my identity."*

A person who is good at something but doesn't like doing it probably is not going to be very effective at that job in the long run. All too frequently, people make the decision to go into law based on one isolated skill that is essential to being a lawyer. Being good at persuading, for example, is a skill frequently called on by lawyers. But there's a lot more to law than persuading. You have to be cognizant of the big picture.

Why Did You Go to Law School?

Here are some of the reasons my clients have given when I ask, *"What made you decide to go to law school?"* Do you recognize yourself in any of these statements?

- I didn't know what else to do.
- I didn't like the sight of blood, so I couldn't be a doctor.
- I'm not good with numbers, so I couldn't go to business school.
- I have a liberal arts degree, and I didn't want to get a PhD and teach.
- All my friends were going.
- I thought it would give me flexibility to do other things.
- I thought I'd make a comfortable income and be financially secure.
- I thought it would be exciting.
- I wanted prestige, status, and to feel important.

- My family thought I would be good at it and encouraged me to go.
- I wanted to help people.
- I thought that [my favorite television show about lawyers] would be an accurate preview of what it would really be like.

So why did YOU go to law school? Was it because you thought you'd excel at the types of skills that lawyers frequently use? Or because your friends or family told you that you'd be good at it? What motivated you?

How Motivated Skills Fit into Your Career Identity

Skills, even motivated skills, are less decisive in the long-term satisfaction of a lawyer than values, psychological needs, and communication style—the first three elements of the career satisfaction model. This is not to say that skills are unimportant. You must be good at something and enjoy it to have career satisfaction. But values and needs are the most important because they are often things that lawyers don't think about, and so they can easily slip off the radar screen. Therefore, they are often out of alignment. Skills, on the other hand, are usually the first thing people consider when choosing a legal career. Lawyers have usually given some thought to their skills. You probably wouldn't have gone into the law if you didn't have some of the skills necessary to become a lawyer.

So it's rare that this element of your career identity will be far off the mark. For example, if you had really wanted to be a physician and would enjoy using a totally different set of skills, why would you have gone into law in the first place? However, it is possible. Take the case of Brenda:

Case study #2. *After college, Brenda studied in France for the profession of her dreams: to be a chef. But her father, a judge, had different ideas, and strongly disapproved. It just didn't seem to him like a legitimate career. So, his daughter dutifully went to law school, and got a job at a large firm. The further she got from her preferred calling, though, the unhappier she became. In desperation, she turned to career counseling…but at first, she didn't mention having abandoned her dream. It was only in the middle of something unrelated that Brenda said that she had written off her dream job as a possibility. I said, "It's so clear you don't want to be a lawyer. The question is, 'Why have you taken chef off the table? Why isn't that one of the options?'" Her response? It felt wrong! When I asked her whose voice that was, she said it was her dad's. I pushed further. "Is it fair," I asked, "To have your dad determine your career? It's your life…not his." Brenda had become a lawyer under family pressure, so it was difficult at first to acknowledge her own desires. But she had a very strong* *motivated skill that was going unfulfilled, and she eventually took ownership of her own career. Though cautious and conservative like so many lawyers, Brenda took several interim steps to take back control of her career…and did achieve her dream of being a chef.*

EXERCISE #1. IDENTIFYING YOUR MOTIVATED SKILLS

Lawyers commonly develop a broad skill set, beginning in law school and continuing throughout their profession. Consider the range of skills you developed in law school, as well as both the data-related and people-related skills frequently called on in the legal profession. Depending on whether you enjoy using your "lawyer" skills, you may or may not find them to be your motivated skills.

In my model, I include both developed skills and innate abilities in this element of your career identity. It doesn't matter how you get good at something, just that you are good at it now and that you enjoy it. When you learn a skill and rehearse it and do it over and over, it's human nature for that to become routinized or "second nature."

In the table below, I have listed a number of common skills, many of them involving work that lawyers do and others that are found outside the law. Circle any words that appeal to you (i.e., they are *both* things that you do well *and* things that you like doing). Don't think too long about any given word or try to assess the possible jobs associated with a word. Just go with your initial instincts about whether the interest described appeals to you.

Achieve goals	Creativity	Forecast	Monitor	Resolve conflict
Act on gut reactions	Critical thinking	Fundraising	Monitor details	Resourcefulness
Active listening	Critical/ precise writing	Gather information	Motivate	Review information
Adapt to new situations	Curiosity	Generate enthusiasm	Musicality	See potential possibilities
Adjudicate	Decision- making	Guide	Negotiate	Sell
Administer	Decisiveness	Identify issues	Notice details	Share
Advise	Dependability	Identify problems	Nurture	Share insights

Agility	Design	Imagination	Object observation	Simplify complexity
Analyze	Detail work	Implement projects	Objectivity	Size-up accurately
Answer questions	Develop expertise	Influence others	Obtain cooperation	Speak
Assist leaders	Develop intimacy	Initiate	Oral advocacy	Stage a production
Athletic ability	Develop programs	Innovate	Oral communication	Strategize
Attention to details	Develop rapport	Inspire others	Organize	Summarize
Brainstorm	Diplomacy	Instruct	Organize groups	Supervise
Budget	Directness	Integrate elements	Paint	Support
Build	Discipline	Intellectual tinkering	Perceive	Synthesize
Calculate	Dispassionate analysis	Interview	Perform	Take inventory
Calm others	Edit	Intuit	Persevere	Take the initiative
Close observation	Educate	Investigate	Persist	Teach
Coach	Efficiency	Lead	Persuade	Team build
Communicate	Empathy	Learn new things	Physical strength	Theorize
Compose	Empirical observation	Learn quickly	Plan	Train
Computer work	Empirical research	Listen	Plan concrete action	Versatility
Conceptualize	Empower others	Logical thinking	Practicality	Visual awareness
Conflict resolution	Entertain	Long-range planning	Pragmatic	Win confidence

Connect people to resources	Establish rapport	Make people laugh	Prioritize	Work under pressure
Consensus building	Evaluate	Make quick decisions	Problem solve	Work with animals
Contemplation	Exercise common sense	Manage	Process information	Work with hands
Coordinate	Experiment	Manage details	Provide expertise	Write
Cost consciousness	Explain	Manage money	Provide feedback	
Counsel	Expressive-ness	Manage people	Public speaking	
Count	Eye/hand coordination	Manage projects	Quick thinking	
Create	Facilitate	Mechanical tinkering	Read	
Create documents	Film	Mediate	Remember details	
Create solutions	Focused concentration	Memory work	Repair	
Creative writing	Follow rules	Mentor	Research	

Add any other skills you might like to use that were not listed above:

_____

_____

_____

_____

_____

_____

_____

_____

_____

EXERCISE #2. PRIORITIZING YOUR MOTIVATED SKILLS

By now, you should have a good idea of the range of your motivated skills. In this next exercise, I will ask you to narrow them down. First, choose your top 10 motivated skills and write them in the spaces below. Again, don't think too long about this exercise. Your first instincts are usually most accurate.

My Top 10 Motivated Skills Are:

_____

_____

_____

_____

_____

_____

_____

_____

_____

_____

Now I want you to narrow your list even further. Of those top 10 motivated skills, which three most appeal to you? Which three would you most want to explore in more depth? I acknowledge the difficulty of choosing only three from the vast universe of possibilities, or even from your list of 10. If you are having trouble selecting just three motivated skills, tell yourself that you are not discarding the others permanently; you are just picking the frontrunners and can go back and sample the others later. Write your top three in the spaces below:

My Top Three Motivated Skills Are:

_____

_____

_____

You have now identified the fourth element of your career identity.

EXERCISE #3. ASSESSING FULFILLMENT OF YOUR MOTIVATED SKILLS

In this final exercise, I will ask you to assess how well your current job fulfills your motivated skills. This should be fairly easy to determine. Take a look at your top three motivated skills. Are they being used in your current job? How about your top ten? Does your current work allow you to use any of them, even tangentially? For each motivated skill, circle whether the skill is being fulfilled or not fulfilled in your current job.

My Top Three Motivated Skills:

_____ [circle one]: Fulfilled/Not Fulfilled

_____ [circle one]: Fulfilled/Not Fulfilled

_____ [circle one]: Fulfilled/Not Fulfilled

My Top 10 Motivated Skills:

_____ [circle one]: Fulfilled/Not Fulfilled

_____ [circle one]: Fulfilled/Not Fulfilled

_____ [circle one]: Fulfilled/Not Fulfilled

_____ [circle one]: Fulfilled/Not Fulfilled

_____ [circle one]: Fulfilled/Not Fulfilled

_____ [circle one]: Fulfilled/Not Fulfilled

_____ [circle one]: Fulfilled/Not Fulfilled

_____ [circle one]: Fulfilled/Not Fulfilled

_____ [circle one]: Fulfilled/Not Fulfilled

_____ [circle one]: Fulfilled/Not Fulfilled

What do you notice about your lists? Are more of your motivated skills currently fulfilled or unfulfilled?

Could I Do That?

In choosing your leading motivated skills, you may have selected some skills you might not be sure you have. How do you know whether you would be good at a skill if you've never done it before? You break the skill into its elements. Take litigation, for example.

What does a litigator do?

Litigators listen to facts, analyze fact situations, and assess and compare those situations to determine whether they've ever been successful in a similar case before. Then, based on facts and research, the litigator constructs legal theories and analyzes those theories. From there, the litigator build arguments based on those theories, and puts them in logical order. Then they discover information from the other side. Litigators also do a lot of writing: motions, pleadings, briefs. They read a lot of things, too. And then they take all that information, and try to convince a trier of fact that their client is right. Litigators employ both intellect and emotions. So, if you were interested in being a litigator, you might ask yourself, "Have I ever analyzed information?" "Have I ever read something for technical meaning?""Have I ever tried to persuade someone to do something?" And so on. You deconstruct the skill into its elements.

> **Case study #6.** *Jeff was a real estate lawyer. He understood and had mastered the real estate laws, and had a successful practice. But he wasn't happy and didn't want to continue to practice law. Jeff just felt that something was missing, and he thought he knew what it was. What Jeff really wanted was to be on the business side of things. He wanted to package the deals. But since he had never been in business or "done deals" before, he didn't know whether he had the necessary skills. So Jeff went to a large real estate developer and told them he wanted to work for them in a business capacity. He proposed and negotiated a deal with the developer, and said that if they didn't think he was doing well on the business side after a trial period they would be free to transfer him to their general counsel's office. The developer agreed. In striking this deal, Jeff actually demonstrated some of the skills that would be needed in his new role.*

I Want to Do That

Some of you may have identified completely new skills that you have never used before, but you would like to use in a career. How do you know whether you could learn the skill adequately to use in a job? It's probably not human nature to enjoy doing something you're not good at. But you may wish you were good at it. Consider the case of Emily:

> **Case study #7.** *Emily loves the Spanish language, and wishes she could speak it better. She's taken classes, but with only moderate success. She probably wouldn't be able to succeed in a career as a translator or interpreter. In this case, though, Emily found a way to use her limited knowledge of Spanish socially by regularly meeting up with other conversational Spanish speakers. This was just enough interaction to satisfy her need to hear and speak the*

language, and is far less than the skill level that would be required of her in a career involving languages.

Now this doesn't mean that you can't acquire a skill, or develop an inborn but latent talent for something. You may find that you need to take more classes, get further training, acquire additional experience, or even obtain another degree or professional certification. For many people, a strong desire to work in a field that uses a particular skill may be just the incentive they need to acquire that skill. For example, suppose a tax lawyer decides after much self-assessment that he really should have been a litigator. If he wants to change practice areas, he will have to develop a different skill set, like the art of taking a deposition, for instance. But if he is motivated to transition to litigation, he will probably be dedicated to acquiring the skills necessary for him to succeed as a litigator. He might take seminars, participate in litigation training clinics, and find himself an experienced mentor.

Additional education and/or training may become even more important if you decide to leave the law altogether:

Case study #8. *After much self-assessment, Peter concluded that he really wanted to become a marriage and family therapist, and that this would be a much better fitting career. Because of his state's licensing laws, though, Peter had to go back to school and obtain a degree in counseling. He took evening classes and spread his schooling out over several years, still practicing law while he completed his degree requirements. Eventually, Peter graduated with a Masters Degree in social work, and opened his own counseling practice. At first, the prospect of returning to school, long hours of study, and an even longer transition were overwhelming, but Peter kept his goal in mind and was ultimately rewarded with a satisfying career.*

You should now have identified your top motivated skills—the fourth element of your career identity. You are almost done! Only one final element of your career identity remains to be discovered—your career interests, which are the subject of the next chapter.

CHAPTER 10

Does Your Job Fit Your Career Interests?

You have now identified four out of the five elements of your career identity—your values, your psychological needs, your communication style, and your motivated interests. In this chapter, we will explore the final component of your career identity—your career interests. Interests are the simplest element of your career identity, and the easiest to figure out. In this chapter, you will have an opportunity to identify and prioritize your main career and vocational interests. Then you can assess how well your job fits your interests.

Do you ever feel bored at work?

Most of us can relate to feeling occasions of boredom or restlessness at some point in our careers. Maybe it's been a slow week, or you have a case of spring fever. But what I'm talking about here is a *persistent boredom,* the feeling that your work is just not inherently interesting to you anymore. If you can identify with this state of mind, it is likely that your job does not meet your career interests. On the other hand, if you feel interested and engaged in the subject matter of your work, then your job probably meets your primary career interests.

Career Interests

Lawyers are sometimes perplexed that their career interests are the last element of The Lawyer Career Satisfaction Model℠, since most generic self-help books tend to place more focus on this area. But one reason for placing career interests last in the model is that people's interests often change over time—sometimes just the degree of interest, and sometimes the subject matter altogether. Of all the elements in career satisfaction, your values are the *least* likely to change while your interests are the *most* likely to change. For that reason, your interests are the least consistent part of your career identity.

Consider the case of Michelle:

Case study #1. *Early in her legal career, Michelle was extremely interested in Constitutional law, and she was sure that she wanted to follow a path that let her sink her teeth into meaty Constitutional amendment issues. So, she took a job as a district attorney and later transitioned to the state attorney general's office, both of which she found fulfilling at the time. At some point, however, Michelle decided to move to a private law firm, and ended up building a practice that consisted entirely of Intellectual Property litigation, which she thoroughly enjoyed. Meanwhile, Michelle got very involved in childhood education advocacy in her community, and she also took a personal interest in emerging businesses in the green economy. At the outset of her career in Constitutional law, Michelle could never have predicted how her interests would change, grow, and evolve.*

Another reason career interests are not introduced earlier is that they reveal only one element of your career identity. Just because you define your interests, you're not home free, as many self-help books would have you believe. In fact, many such books invite the reader to make comprehensive lists of all their interests since childhood, and then pick a career that fits all those interests. Most people look at their list of disparate interests and wonder, *"What do I do with this information? I don't have any idea what job fits all of my interests."* Exactly. Because it's unlikely any job is going to bind together all your many interests, which is one reason that trying to choose a profession based on a list of them will lead you astray. Take Lauren, for example:

Case study #2. *Lauren, a dissatisfied lawyer, knew that she didn't want to practice law anymore but wasn't sure what direction to go. So she pored through a half-dozen of the most popular career books and, as suggested, made a list of all the things that interested her. Here is what she came up with: books and writing; travel; animals; interior design; fashion; real estate; foreign languages; psychology; the arts; food and wine; philosophy; teaching; coaching/consulting; ballroom dancing; tennis; skiing; rowing; and fencing. In looking over her list of interests, Lauren became even more confused about their application toward a career. Should she dabble in a few of these interests, trying various jobs on for fit? Or was she destined to end up unfulfilled if she didn't get a job that used all her interests?*

Obviously, no one career is going to fit all of Lauren's interests under one big tent. In fact, it would be challenging for her to try to combine more than a couple of them. Lauren's list may seem long, but people often have many varied interests—even if some are still unexplored. So, expecting to find a career that fulfills all or even most of them is unrealistic and an exercise in frustration. So after you complete the exercises below and identify your interests, don't despair if you don't see a way to link them all together under one professional umbrella.

EXERCISE #1. IDENTIFYING YOUR INTERESTS

The world of possible interests is infinite. I have listed some common interests below, many of which are shared by other lawyers, and others that are found in the general population. Circle any words that appeal to you. As with the list of motivated skills in Chapter 9, don't think too long about any given word or try to assess the possible jobs associated with a word. Just go with your initial instincts about whether the interest described appeals to you.

Accounting	Cultures	How things work	Medicine	Religion
Acting	Current events	Human behavior	Modern jazz	Real estate
Animal rights	Design	Human motivation	Morality	Rhetoric
Animals	Ecology	Human potential	Movies	Science
Anthropology	Economics	Human relations	Music	Science fiction
Antiques	Education	Human rights	Music therapy	Securities
Architecture	Electronics	Indigenous cultures	Musicians	Self-help
Art	Entertaining	Information	Mysteries	Skiing
Astro-physics	Environment	Inner city problems	Mythology	Social issues
Athletics	Fads/trends	Insurance	Nature	Social justice
Bankruptcy	Fantasy	Intellectual property	Nutrition	Social science
Bicycling	Fashion	Interior design	Organizational psychology	Sociopathic behavior

Books	Fiction	International law	Other cultures	Software applications
Business	Finance	Inventions	Outdoors	Spirituality
Career choices	Fine arts	Investments	Parenting	Sports
Children	Fitness	Irony	People	Swimming
Civil rights	Food	Elder issues	Philosophy	Technology
Classical ballet	Foreign cultures	Journalism	Photography	Television
Community activism	Foreign	Jurisprudence	Physics	Decision-making process
Computers	Foreign trade	Labor law	Physiology	The past
Constitutional law	Furniture	Language	Poetry	The unusual
Consumer protection	Gardening	Law	Political satire	Toys
Cooking	Group dynamics	Legal theory	Politics	Travel industry
Crafts	Health	Lifestyles	Poverty law	Wilderness
Criminal law	History	Literature	Psychology	Women's issues
Criminal psychology	History of law	Magazines	Public issues	Words
Criminality	Horses	Math	Public policy	Work safety
Culinary arts	Housing	Mechanical things	Publishing	Youth

Now, add any other interests of your own that were not listed above:

_____

_____

_____

_____

_____

_____

_____

EXERCISE #2. PRIORITIZING YOUR INTERESTS

By now, you should have a good idea of the range of your interests. In this next exercise, I will ask you to narrow them down. First, choose your top ten interests and write them in the spaces below. Again, don't think too long about this exercise. Your first instincts are usually most accurate.

My Top 10 Interests Are:

_____

_____

_____

_____

_____

_____

_____

_____

_____

_____

Now I want you to narrow down your list even further. Of those top 10 interests, which three appeal to you most? Which three would you most want to explore in more depth? I appreciate the difficulty of choosing only three from the vast universe of possibilities, or even from your list of ten. If you are having trouble selecting just three interests, tell yourself that you are not discarding the others permanently; you are just picking the frontrunners and can go back and sample the others later. Write your top three in the spaces below:

My Top Three Interests Are:

_____

_____

_____

You have now identified the final element of your career identity.

EXERCISE #3. ASSESSING INTERESTS FULFILLMENT

In this final exercise, I will ask you to assess how well your current job fulfills your career interests. This should be fairly easy to determine. Take a look at your top three interests. Are they being met in your current job? How about your top ten? Does your current work involve any of them, even tangentially? For each interest, circle whether the interest is fulfilled or not fulfilled in your current job.

My Top Three Interests:

_____ [circle one]: Fulfilled/Not Fulfilled

_____ [circle one]: Fulfilled/Not Fulfilled

_____ [circle one]: Fulfilled/Not Fulfilled

My Top 10 Interests:

_____ [circle one]: Fulfilled/Not Fulfilled

_____ [circle one]: Fulfilled/Not Fulfilled

_____ [circle one]: Fulfilled/Not Fulfilled

_____ [circle one]: Fulfilled/Not Fulfilled

_____ [circle one]: Fulfilled/Not Fulfilled

_____ [circle one]: Fulfilled/Not Fulfilled

_____ [circle one]: Fulfilled/Not Fulfilled

_____ [circle one]: Fulfilled/Not Fulfilled

_____ [circle one]: Fulfilled/Not Fulfilled

_____ [circle one]: Fulfilled/Not Fulfilled

What do you notice about your lists? Are more of your interests currently fulfilled or unfulfilled? If none of your top three interests—or very few of your top ten interests—are not currently being met in your job, don't get discouraged. As I will discuss below, interests are not king when it comes to job satisfaction. That's not to say that they are unimportant. Obviously, you want to be interested, not bored, with your work. However, interests alone, as you will see, are not a reliable indicator of whether you would find satisfying work in that particular field.

Interests Alone Are Not Sufficient

Now that you have identified and prioritized your career interests, remember this: your interests alone are not a sufficient basis for a career choice.

> **Case study #3.** *Bill was an unhappy trial lawyer who started seeing a career counselor. One of several vocational tests concluded that he would be happier as an airline flight attendant. It didn't matter that Bill had little desire to work in this area, but the test was based on his interests, which included a desire to help people from a diverse population, to work in a unique setting, to travel to exotic locations, and to use his foreign language skills. You could see how a vocational test might conclude that this unhappy lawyer would be happier as a flight attendant. But once Bill looked at the totality of his career identify—his values, psychological needs, communication style, and motivated skills—he realized that while his interests fit the job...that was all. And if he had chosen a career in aviation based just on his interests, he would have ended up very dissatisfied and wondering what went wrong.*

Interests can be misleading. You might think that your interests would be a good fit for a particular job, but maybe the reality of the job doesn't make much use of those interests. This comes up often for law students in deciding which area of practice in which to specialize. Skills and interests are the two things that many law students use as criteria, probably because they are two of the most salient characteristics of a job and thus easily evaluated. The questions law students ask themselves about their prospective careers usually follow along the lines of, *Do I want to be a litigator or a transactional lawyer? Do I want to work in real estate or environmental law?* However, taking a class in trusts and estates and finding it interesting is no guarantee that you will also find an estate planning practice stimulating.

> **Case study #4.** *Matt was a third-year law student who decided that he wanted to develop a practice in entertainment law. He found his entertainment law class the most interesting of all his classes, and he looked forward to an exciting career working with other entertainment industry professionals. But if Matt was honest with himself, he would have admitted to thinking that he was going to get to hang out with celebrities, and maybe even have his own brush with greatness. The problem is that Entertainment law is not very entertaining; it's basically contract law. It was misleading for Matt to select a practice area based solely on his interest in a particular subject as it was presented in law school. He would no doubt find the day-to-day realities of the profession far less interesting.*

If you look at your interests in a vacuum and don't consider all the elements of your career identity, you can be led astray into choosing a job that would actually be a very bad fit for you.

HOW ARE INTERESTS RELATED TO PASSIONS?

Is a passion just a very strong interest?

There's a lot of discussion in career self-help books about finding your passion, or doing what you love. I like to say that passions are interests on steroids. Passions are interests taken to the nth degree. If you recall the career anchor we discussed in Chapter 6, one of the Career Anchors is called Craft, which means, "I really love the nature of the work itself. I am the craft. Who I am is a lawyer. Or who I am is a writer, or an actor, or a chef, or whatever the work may be. I just can't imagine doing anything else." If you feel this way, you've got to follow your passion.

If you are passionate about something, you likely already know it. Sometimes, people will discover their passion from reading a career book. Something the author says sparks something in the reader. Usually, though, career passions emerge naturally. If you are one of these people who are passionate about something, then hopefully this book will help you figure out how to translate your passion into a satisfying career.

The fly in the ointment is that only about 10 percent of people like something to the point that it becomes a passion. There's so much publicity in our society about people who have found their passion. It gives the rest of us the impression that all we need to do is figure out what we're passionate about and everything will fall into place. The truth is that 90 percent of us aren't going to find that passion in our work. We may find it in a hobby, or we may not. We may just be interested in many things, no single one of which claims an exclusive hold on our passions. Or our interests may change over our lifetime, waxing and waning at different intervals. The majority of people just won't feel that intensity about one thing to which they want to devote their entire career. Most of us will need to find some other basis on which to choose our careers.

Don't despair if you are in this 90 percent. I've got good news for you. You have as much of a chance of finding career satisfaction as anyone else. Satisfaction is the goal you should be striving for, and if you do the exercises in this book, you are well on your way to finding it.

You have now explored all five elements of your career identity. In Section III, you will see exactly how all these elements fit together, and you will map out your strategy for finding career satisfaction.

SECTION III
WHERE ARE YOU GOING?

Chapter 11   Identifying Your Ideal Job   *90*

Chapter 12   The Case for Solo Practice   *103*

Chapter 13   Finding Work Inside, Outside & Around the Law   *111*

Chapter 14   Putting Your Best Foot Forward   *124*

Chapter 15   The Personal Obstacles to Career Satisfaction   *134*

Chapter 16   Should I Leave the Law?   *143*

Chapter 17   The Disengagement Process   *146*

Chapter 18   Your Support Network   *160*

CHAPTER 11

Identifying Your Ideal Job

This section explores the different categories of jobs available to you as a legal professional, and how to evaluate the fit between your career identity and a job.

You should come away from these exercises with an understanding of your job criteria—what you must have in a job, what you would like to have, and what you must avoid if you are to achieve job satisfaction. After you have identified your job criteria and ideal job, I will walk you through the entire job search process, from identifying potential employers to using your contacts to your full advantage. I will also discuss the additional factors to consider if you want to work for yourself. Next we will tackle some of the thorniest objections that lawyers in transition face out in the job market. Finally, I will explain what to expect during a transition and how you can boost your odds of making a successful job or career change. You are in the home stretch of your journey!

In career counseling, one of a client's inevitable first questions is, *How long does it take to make a career transition?* After more than 15 years counseling lawyers, I can tell you this: the length of time depends on how big a change you want to make, and how far you want to go from your current position.

Consider:

- If you want to stay in the law, expect your job search to last at least six months.
- If you want to move to a law-related field, you could be looking at six months to a year or two, depending on whether additional training or certification is necessary.
- If you want to leave the law altogether, you should expect a multi-step transition process that could last several years.

In each case, you can expect your transition to take longer than you think… and it will usually involve a reduction in income—especially in a down economy. Author Tom Jackson once wrote a book that depicts what he says is a typical career transition process. His illustration was fairly simple: the entire page consisted of a single word—*NO*—repeated endlessly until you got to the bottom of the page, where the last word was *YES*. Jackson's point was that when you look for work—or your career is up in the air—you may get many "no's" before you get that one "yes".

One of the difficulties of changing careers is the psychological transition that is required. To shift from practicing law to a whole new career, you almost always have to go back a few steps and enter the workforce at a level lower than someone with your experience would expect. It's not a pleasant feeling, which is why so many lawyers and other professionals resist it. You think to yourself, "*I'm a lawyer. I should be able to get a job just like that.*" It doesn't usually work that way. However, as you get closer to what's right for you, as you learned in the previous five chapters, things do change for the better. Your career-change process begins to pick up speed, and your situation feels more hopeful. Having learned your career identity, you have more experience, more confidence, and more direction.

So let's begin: what category of work will best fit your career identity?

Job Categories

Given the seemingly unlimited field of possibilities, how do you determine which career would best fit your career identity? It may seem overwhelming, but you can actually streamline your decision by first separating the job world into three categories:

a. Jobs that involve staying in the law
b. Jobs that are law-related
c. Jobs that have nothing to do with the law

a. You want to stay in the law. The first category—and the easiest transition to make—has you making one or more adjustments so that you can remain in the law. After all, you basically enjoy the work that lawyers do, and you want that to continue. And yet, having learned more about your career identity, you feel there is something about where or how you are doing the work that is not a good fit. So, the challenge now is to look at which job setting will fit you best.

Consider these options:

You decide to change firms

- Different size
- Different client base
- Different culture or supervising partner

You decide to change geographical setting

- Urban vs. suburban vs. rural
- Different town, city, state, or country

You decide to change practice area

You decide to change working conditions (e.g., reduced hours; telecommute; job share)

You decide to change work setting (e.g., doing legal work other than in a law firm)

- Government
- Corporate legal department
- Legal aid, legal services, public defender offices
- Nonprofit organizations, foundations, community organizations
- Bar associations
- Universities and other educational institutions
- Pre-paid legal plans
- Legal clinics and nationwide "law firms"
- Military
- Labor union

Many lawyers think they have to leave the law to find career satisfaction. But once they do their self-assessment, it may become clear that they really only need to make a minor modification.

Depending on which elements of your career identity are out of alignment, you probably already have some clues about how to modify your situation in a way that would improve your job satisfaction. So, here's my suggestion: since you have already decided that you still want to be a lawyer, your *motivated skills* are probably not an issue (unless you want to switch from a litigation practice to a transactional practice or vice versa). If your *communication style* doesn't fit with those of your colleagues, a change in firm would probably help (or possibly a change in work setting or geographical setting). If your *career interests* are not being met, then a change in practice area might be appropriate. And if some of your *values* and/or *psychological needs* are not a good fit with your current work situation, then any of the above changes just might be the necessary adjustment, depending on the particular value or psychological need.

b. You want to move to a law-related job. The second category—and the next easiest transition to make—is to change to a law-related job.

Let's say that more than one element of your career identity is out of alignment, and you have determined that merely making a change within the profession would not be enough to provide you with greater job satisfaction. And yet, there are some things about the law or working with lawyers that you do enjoy, and you don't want to leave the legal field altogether. In that case, you could change to a job where you will not be practicing law, but can use your law background in some direct way. Law-related jobs come in so many different flavors (see Appendix A, *800+ Ways to Use Your Law Degree*). Numerous industries are connected to the legal profession.

So what is it that would make you attractive to an employer in a law-related industry? Generally speaking, you can make a successful transition to a law-related job by transferring your legal skills, your substantive expertise, your general knowledge or understanding of the legal profession, or your contacts. Let's look at skills first. For example, if you're a lawyer and a good writer or editor, that might be enough to get you a job with a legal publisher. If you also have a degree in journalism, English, or communications, that would improve your chances even more, but it's not always necessary.

> **Case study #1.** *Kathryn practiced law as an associate in a midsized firm doing general business law. After a few years, she transitioned to a job as an associate editor for a financial publishing company where she wrote summaries of case law on business valuation. A few years later, she turned to freelance editing for her state bar association's newsletter, and eventually became the bar's full-time editor. Kathryn did not have an educational background in writing. However, she had served as an editor of law review and honed her writing skills in various positions. Her undergraduate degree in finance and experience in business law also carried weight with the financial publisher.*

Some law-related jobs are appropriate for anyone with typical experience as a lawyer; others are more appropriate for someone with a background in a specific substantive area: an employment lawyer might go into human resources;

an estate planning lawyer might transition into financial advisory services; a real estate lawyer might go into commercial real estate development; and so on. Certain specialty jobs that are law-related are available only in particular geographic areas; jobs like legislative aide, lobbyist, or legislative analyst are primarily available only in Washington, D.C. or in a state capital.

> **Case study #2.** *Linda got her initial legal experience in the labor and employment law practice group of a large firm. She knew she didn't want to stay there long-term, but she used her time there to gain valuable expertise that would translate to the private sector. One of Linda's clients hired her as in-house counsel, focusing on the company's personnel issues. Later, she transitioned again, this time to a management position as human resources director of an international sports apparel company.*

Your general knowledge of the legal profession and understanding of how lawyers work may also provide you a basis for transitioning to a law-related job. Organizational consulting, career coaching or counseling, state bar associations, law school administration, and professional development positions in law firms are all examples of positions or employers that would draw on a general knowledge of and experience in the legal profession.

> **Case Study #3.** *After spending several years in general private practice, Scott left the law to run the publications department of a publisher of business and finance books. Rejoining the legal world again a few years later, he went to work for a legal publisher and seminar developer, where he managed the various projects and created new products and training programs for lawyers and law firms.*

Your legal contacts alone might make you valuable to a law-related employer. Sales organizations like West Publishing (a division of Thomson Reuters), or facilities management companies, or litigation service providers and the like, hire lawyers with law firm contacts so they can introduce their products or services. The companies aren't interested in your legal skills or knowledge; they just want to know that you can open doors for them.

> **Case Study #4.** *Nicole worked in a midsize firm doing mostly defense litigation work. She also used her marketing background to promote her husband's restaurant. Nicole left her firm to free up more time for the marketing and started her own practice doing a mix of business and criminal cases. In her search for a new career direction, she met and joined forces with a speaker and*

consultant who specialized in nonverbal communications. Leveraging Nicole's
diverse background and contacts in the legal profession, they teamed up to offer
jury consulting services to lawyers and law firms.

Finally, you might also consider additional education or certification. In a tight and frustrating job market, your investment in retraining tells potential employers that you're dedicated and committed to your new career of choice, and not just looking for an escape from the law. It doesn't have to be another four-year degree; it could be just a credentialing program in the new field (note: see Appendix B and the sidebar at the end of this chapter).

c. You want to leave the law (also see chapters 14 and 16). The third category—and the longest, most difficult career transition to make—is to leave the law altogether and to go into an unrelated industry.

Let's say that your self-assessment has made it clear to you that all aspects of your career identity are out of alignment, and that even a law-related job is not enough to produce greater job satisfaction. You no longer want to use your legal skills, expertise, knowledge of the profession, or contacts; you are clear that you want to move in an entirely different direction. So how do you leave the law, and adopt a completely new career?

Case study #5. *Rachel did a lot of litigation surrounding women's health issues, but she was a litigator who didn't like conflict. She preferred the intellectual challenge of litigation, and was very good at mastering a lot of scientific facts involving women's healthcare. In an analysis of her career, Rachel realized that she was really good at taking a complex medical issue, and explaining it in a way that people were interested and could understand it. In fact, very often she found herself in the role of teacher, educating clients, juries, and judges about some technical scientific or medical issue. In our counseling work together, Rachel realized that she wanted a job that would allow her to teach women's medical issues, and to use her analytical, verbal, and teaching skills without the drama of courtroom conflict. So, she decided to approach pharmaceutical companies, which often sponsor public educational programs to promote their products. Rachel analyzed the field and approached two companies, making her case to each: that women are injured using their products, and every time a lawsuit is filed it costs the company money even if they win. Hiring her to educate women would not only be less expensive, but would reduce liability and create goodwill and greater exposure to the company's product. One of the companies loved Rachel's proposal, and hired her. The end result was a job that was much more satisfying for her than her work as a trial lawyer.*

Moving to a job in another field outside of law is a process that often requires multiple steps. If your goal is to leave the law entirely, it will require considerable research, informational interviewing, creative thinking…and you'll doubtless have to repackage yourself. First, you need to make a transition away from what you've been doing and toward something you want (see Appendix A). Your new first job may not be the ideal, but you need to build your skills and continue to zigzag in the direction you want to go. It's not unlike sailing a boat, tacking first to one side and then another with a firm eye on the horizon. A good example of a two-step transition are lawyers who change from private practice to in-house counsel, and who continue to work in the same substantive area. Once they are in-house, they are able to transition into a business or compliance role. They are usually able to make this switch to the client side because they have built up relationships with their clients over the years.

If you decide to leave the law, I recommend you read chapters 14 and 16 as part of your research.

THERE ARE MORE CREDENTIALS THAN AN LL.M.

Certificate programs offer an opportunity to obtain a credential—often a very strong one—with far less investment of time and money than for an LL.M.

For example, for an investment of about $1,000 and a few months time, you can earn a prestigious Associate in Risk Management (ARM) credential, completing the three levels of courses and three examinations online at your convenience! Once you have an ARM credential to accompany your JD, you become a serious candidate for corporate risk management positions. Between 20-25 percent of U.S. risk managers possess a JD degree. In fact, U.S. law schools currently offer more than 30 certificate programs in more than 25 topic areas that are open to non-degree (JD or LL.M. candidates). What's more, a growing number of these programs are available online.

In addition to law school certificate programs, many non-law school academic institutions, as well as trade and professional associations and private companies, offer legal and law-related certificate programs, both onsite and online. There are at least 400 such programs in approximately 60 practice areas that might be suitable for you, depending on your interests and career aspirations. Expand your research into credential-enhancing programs to include law-related ones. Depending upon your background and interests, and the state of the job market in your area, you may be better off in terms of enhancing your legal employability if you obtain a law-related graduate degree or a law-related professional certificate instead of an LL.M.

These days, with increasing pressure from clients to cut costs and run more efficiently, law firms are increasingly turning to Project Management as a methodology by which they can increase the efficiency with which matters are handled. There is an existing field of Project Management, with several certifying entities, that you may want to explore if your personality naturally fits with efficiently managing projects.

Below are some due diligence guidelines that will help you make an intelligent selection:

Talk to individuals who have already earned the credential. Get their opinions as to whether the credential made a difference to their legal careers, employability, promotion potential and compensation. Ask them:

How difficult was it to find suitable employment after completing the program?
How much help—and what kind of help—did you receive with respect to finding employment from the granting institution's career and/or program office?
If you had it to do over again, would you still pursue the credential—again?

Talk to employers of individuals who have recently earned the credential. Ask them:

Do you value the fact that your employee has the credential?
How does the credential benefit your organization?
Would you have hired the employee absent the credential?
Do you believe the credential is a career booster?
What is your opinion of the various credential-granting organizations?

Talk to current students. Ask them:

Is the program worth the time, effort, money, and career interruption?
What do they intend to do with their degree or certificate?
How much, and what is the nature of the career assistance they are receiving from the granting institution?

Talk to the career placement professionals and program directors at the sponsoring school or organization. This is the most important due diligence element of all. Ask them:

Where can I expect to work once I successfully complete the program?
What is the institution's track record when it comes to placing program graduates?

Where do recent graduates work and what career paths will be open to me?

What are the specifics of what you can do for me during, and after I complete, the program?

By Richard L. Hermann, Esq.

Excerpt: *From Lemons to Lemonade in the New Legal Job Market* (LawyerAvenue Press, 2012)

Note: See Appendix B for a list of legal and law-related certificate and credential-building programs.

Your Job Environment

Your choice of job category and type of job should not be the end of your efforts. In fact, it may not even be the most important thing you do. Do you remember the Career Anchors model from Chapter 6? Research from this model suggests that for most of us, our source of job satisfaction comes from something *other* than identifying the right line of work or even job category. For most of us, *job environment* is as important—if not more important—than the type of job in determining ultimate job satisfaction. For most lawyers, the environmental conditions are more determinative of job satisfaction.

> **Case study #6.** *Consider James, a lawyer who decided he wanted to switch careers and become an executive recruiter. Identifying "recruiter" as his job choice answers the question of what type of job he should do. But it doesn't tell him what job would be most satisfying. Maybe the job choice meets some of James' interests and skills criteria, but the first three criteria—his values, psychological needs, and communication style—are much more likely to be salient in determining not only what career or job he chooses, but in guiding him towards the particular employer and working conditions within that job choice.*

What else does James need to ask himself? He needs to know what sort of recruiting position he wants…what sort of company he wants to work for… what sort of boss he would work well with…how much autonomy would he have…and the culture or workplace climate that would fit his career identity. James might be able to choose from a dozen different recruiting jobs, ranging on a spectrum from "I hate my job" to "I love my job." They're all recruiting jobs. So, just knowing that James wants to be a recruiter isn't likely by itself to give him the job satisfaction he wants. He needs to know more about the job's environment; that's really where the first three elements of his career identity are likely to intersect.

Take autonomy, for example. Autonomy is one of the values lawyers hold to a greater degree than does the general public. If James places a strong value on a high degree of autonomy, and he ends up working for a micro-managing, obsessive-compulsive boss, he'll quickly hate the job even though the nature of the work plays to his strengths. Because that one value (autonomy) is so important to him, it would trump everything else.

Case study #7. *Sarah is a good example why job environment is so important. Sarah was a public finance specialist for a big law firm. At first, she thought she wanted to leave the law because she felt the work was drudgery, her co-workers were small-minded, and the firm's meetings stifling. She couldn't stand working there (she often checked her watch hoping for the end of the day), and she often wondered if getting a JD had been a mistake. In the course of our career counseling work, Sarah's complaints turned out to be environmental in nature, and unrelated to practicing law or the nature of her specialty. In conversation, she said that before joining her firm she had been excited about the field of public finance, and that the nature of the work still interested her. Indeed, Sarah's assessed values, psychological needs, and communication style pointed to being a fit for the type of work she was doing...just NOT in her law firm's culture. So, she talked to a public finance specialist at another firm where the culture was quite different. With her contacts there, Sarah accepted a job offer and rediscovered what had always excited her about the law. But if she hadn't paused to factor job environment into the equation, her story might have ended quite differently.*

By identifying your most important values, psychological needs, communication style, skills, and interests, you can go a long way towards identifying the kind of total work experience that you need for long-term career satisfaction. But it is knowing what kind of daily experience you want to have at work that will help you assess whether a particular type of job and job environment is likely to consistently provide that experience.

EXERCISE #1. THE IDEAL JOB GRID

In this exercise, you are going to create a more complete picture of your ideal job criteria. You will identify what you must have, what you would like to have, and what you must avoid—for each of the five elements of your career identity, as well as for your job environment. Review your answers to the exercises in chapters 6 through 10, as well as any of the bonus exercises that you did from Appendix D. Highlight words and phrases that appear repeatedly in the exercises. Place those words and phrases in the appropriate category. Make sure you put something in every category, and aim for a few words or phrases in each. If you have trouble narrowing down your lists, experiment with different versions.

	Must Have	*Would Like*	*Must Avoid*
Values			
Needs			
Communication Style			
Motivated Skills			
Career Interests			
Job Environment			

EXERCISE #2. CAREER COUNSELOR RECOMMENDATIONS

In this exercise, you are going to take on the role of career counselor to yourself. Look at the job criteria you identified above in your ideal job grid. Consider the patterns and themes that identify what would really make you happy in your work. Take everything you've learned about yourself into account. *Now,* write a report as if you're the career counselor and someone has come to you and presented you this information on yourself. Write the report from the position of a third-party objective analyst. (For example, you might write, *"I recommend that Terry consider a job that . . . "*). Summarize the patterns that you see, and finish with a recommendation section on what you recommend for yourself. Be as specific as you possibly can. Address not only the job category and job title within that category, but also describe the job environment, including the geographic setting, work setting, work culture, and working conditions.

Report for: [your name] _____

Observations: _____

_____

_____

_____

Recommendations:

_____

_____

_____

_____

EXERCISE #3. MISSION STATEMENT

In this exercise, you are going to write a mission statement for your ideal job—your vision of exactly what you are looking for. It is very important that you be extremely clear about the position you are seeking even though this is a hypothetical first effort. The greatest success you're going to have is going to come from connections with people you already know. And the only way you can get those connections to work for you is to have a very clear vision—so that when you describe it, people instantly understand and remember it. You are creating a mental picture of your ideal job.

People are often afraid to choose just one job or to be too specific in writing their mission statement, in case they find something else that works. They don't want to close off any opportunities. But the twist is that picking a goal won't prevent you from finding something else. In fact, it often helps you find something else, however odd that may seem. The reality is that being goal-directed and focused opens doors to all kinds of opportunities beyond the goal itself, whereas people who are vague about what they want have a very hard time getting any traction. So don't be afraid to get specific!

Sample Mission Statement #1:

My ideal job is to work for the U.S. Government as a Foreign Service Officer in North Africa, specializing in cultural affairs. I want to use my proficiency in French, my skills in diplomacy, and my interest in geopolitics to create connections between the United States and cultural institutions in the region. I want to work in a physically secure office and a collaborative work environment. I want to work with colleagues who enjoy socializing together and discussing broad foreign policy issues, and who support each other with the demands of expatriate life.

Sample Mission Statement #2:

My ideal job is to work as a university guidance counselor at a small liberal arts college in the South. I want to have daily contact with students, and be involved in a wide range of issues, from advising them on career options and arranging for graduate study programs to providing a sounding board for personal concerns. I want to work and live in a small community with a slower pace of living that is centered on campus life. I want to develop close personal bonds with other faculty, who share my love of learning and commitment to student development. I want to work for a college that is well-funded and respects tradition, yet values innovative thinking.

My Mission Statement:

_____

_____

_____

_____

Congratulations! If you took on the exercises in this chapter, you have succeeded in putting together all the pieces of a complex puzzle—you! You have taken the various elements of your career identity, developed your job criteria, and considered which job category and environment would be a good fit. That's no small task! Not only that, but you have identified your ideal job and crafted detailed recommendations for yourself, along with a mission statement that will prove invaluable to you as you begin networking. You are now well down the road from where you began…and well on your way to finding job satisfaction.

CHAPTER 12

The Case for Solo Practice

Solo practice remains one of the best-kept secrets of the legal profession because no one bothers to make a strong case in its defense. Until now. In this chapter, an excerpt from Carolyn Elefant's *Solo by Choice 2011/2012*, you'll find seven powerful arguments for starting your own firm:

Argument #1. Autonomy

When I ask solos to identify the strongest reasons for starting their own practice, the one at the top of nearly everyone's list is…*autonomy*. It doesn't surprise me. In contrast to other professions, a law practice, by its very nature, demands deference: as lawyers, we serve clients, we're bound by precedent, we're constricted by a code of professional ethics. So, when you add such factors as the bureaucracy of a law firm or government practice…and firm hierarchy and the rigidity of a partnership track…*and* the ego-driven tendency of many lawyers to want to do things "my way," it's only natural that some lawyers crave the freedom that comes with solo'ing:

Freedom to choose cases. Above all, starting a practice liberates lawyers from the overbearing bureaucracy of practicing law in any kind of a large entity, be it a big firm, inside a corporation, or at a government agency. Within these organizations, most lawyers have no control over the cases they're assigned, and usually the younger or less-favored attorneys wind up either with the duds or more mundane tasks within a matter. Associates don't get much relief even when they take the initiative to drum up their own clients. Even when an associate gets a nibble from a potential client, he or she still needs to discuss the prospect with a supervisor or write up a proposal to a committee to justify taking on the client. And many times, firms turn away the types of clients that younger associates attract, either because the clients can't afford the firm fees, or they create a conflict with the firm's larger, institutional clients.

By contrast, solos don't have this problem.

Solos can pick exactly the types of cases they want to handle, and develop their very own strategy to handle them. And at the end of the day, even though lawyers with their own practice may need to consult with their partners, or decide to seek guidance from a more experienced lawyer in making decisions about the merits of a case or pursuing a particular strategy, the decision to accept a case is theirs alone.

Not only does autonomy eliminate frustration and sense of powerlessness, it also gives solos an edge over their large-firm counterparts. Solos run their own ship, and they're the best situated to act quickly when a novel or new matter crosses their path. And because most successful solos have a propensity for risk, they're also not scared off by the prospect of taking a case that involves an area of law with which they have little or no experience. Contrast the solo mentality to that of a large firm, where a new client matter involving a unique or complicated legal question of first impression would require an endless litany of conflict tests, committee meetings, and preliminary (but still exhaustive) associate research before the firm would make a decision on whether to accept the case. By that time, the client would probably have sought other counsel.

In just one example, small-firm lawyer Tom Goldstein, who specializes in Supreme Court litigation, beat out several other large firms to snag a compelling death penalty matter. Why? Goldstein was able to decide to accept the case after consulting with his law partner, who happened to be his wife. In fact, Goldstein was already on a plane to Tennessee to meet the client while the large firms were still deliberating over whether to accept the matter. (Note: Goldstein has since moved to a large firm, where he serves as partner while his wife continues to operate their former practice with another lawyer.)

Lawyers in solo practice can also structure a firm that's conducive to the types of cases they want to take on. For example, one lawyer I know started his own firm after he grew tired of his BigLaw employer turning down potentially precedent-setting appellate matters that he brought to the practice because the prospective clients couldn't afford the firm's hourly rates. As a solo, the lawyer opened an office in a suburban location closer to his home, and invested in the right combination of hardware and software that he could manage most administrative tasks without a full-time assistant. As a result, he was able to take on cases that his former firm declined as unprofitable. Even more satisfying, he's earning more money than he ever did at the firm.

There's also the experience of North Carolina solo Stephanie Kimbro, who started one of the first virtual law practices, i.e., an entirely Internet-based law firm. As a young associate, Kimbro noticed that her firm frequently turned away small transactional matters because they weren't cost-effective. So after her daughter was born, Kimbro and her husband created an online system that enabled Kimbro to work with clients exclusively online and streamline the workflow with forms. The increased efficiencies allowed Kimbro to economically serve the smaller clients that her former firm once turned away.

Freedom in handling cases. These days, most large organizations don't exactly encourage recommendations on case strategy from associates. In fact, conventional wisdom advises associates to *refrain* from offering suggestions about potential case theories since the partners have likely already considered them anyway. And in a tight economy, where associates fear for their jobs, there's more incentive than ever to avoid rocking the boat.

Freedom from office politics. In many ways, working for others resembles a giant rite of passage. To get ahead, you've got to feign enthusiasm over sleep-inducing research projects or contribute money to a partner's favored charity. As Stephen Harper, a former BigLaw partner writes: "… *Those at the top wield power that makes or breaks young careers, and everybody knows it. Doing a superior job is important, but working for the 'right' people is outcome determinative.*" Solo practice liberates you from just this sort of foolish, often degrading, demonstrations of hierarchy and power, leaving you free to actually practice law not inter-office politics.

Freedom over small matters. While most solos revel in their autonomy over substantive matters, sometimes it's just the freedom to make decisions about the smallest, most trivial things that makes the biggest difference. When I started my own practice, I made a point of choosing office supplies distinct from the standard issue at my former law firm—such as choosing Post-Its in bright pink instead of corporate yellow; expensive pens not cheap ball-points; business cards with blue print-on-cream rather than black-on-white. Not necessarily because I preferred them...but because I could.

Argument #2. Practical Experience

With corporate clients barring entry-level associates from handling their matters, and partners hoarding work, law firms no longer provide many opportunities for new associates to gain hands-on experience. When you establish your own law firm, it's you who gets the experience. For example, if you bring a business client with you from your former firm, you—and not the partner—will negotiate and draft the company's next contract. If it's an appellate matter, it's you who writes the brief and argues the case. And when the client calls for advice—on anything from a pressing strategic decision to how to dress for a deposition—it's your advice he or she wants because there's no one else. Solo practice also gives you opportunities to gain practical experience in new fields. *Author note:* When I started my firm, I'd been out of law school for five years and had never set foot in a courtroom except to observe. However, my practice specialty—energy regulatory work—didn't give me opportunity for trial work since most regulatory disputes are resolved on the papers or perhaps at an administrative hearing. So, to get the court time I craved, I signed up for court-appointed criminal cases. Within six months, I had a bench trial and argued a couple of motions, and within a year had my first jury trial. I never would have had those opportunities if I remained at a law firm, especially in my practice area.

Argument #3. To Feel Like a Lawyer

Back in the 19th Century, Karl Marx decried the Industrial Revolution for alienating workers from the product of their labor. He argued that where once craftsmen built a product from start to finish, the assembly line had atomized the process for the sake of efficiency, robbing the working class of the satisfaction of their craft. Sound familiar? In some ways, modern American law firms resemble the assembly lines Marx so vigorously condemned. At large firms, lawyers—primarily associates—work only on portions of a case, often never speaking with a client or even being privy to the entire matter. In fact, many lawyers today feel like paper-pushers, sleep-walking through their jobs rather than being vibrant professionals with the ability to solve problems and make a difference in people's lives.

On the other hand, solo practice makes you feel like a real lawyer, the kind of lawyer you imagined you would be back in law school. And each time you introduce yourself in the courtroom or boardroom; each time you reassure a nervous client; each time you explain to prospective clients what you can do for them, you reinforce the image of yourself as an autonomous, can-do professional with the tools to solve problems, resolve disputes, and even improve the legal system. And that feeling of being a lawyer never goes away, even when you're handling such administrative tasks as photocopying your own briefs or sending out bills late at night, because those tasks aren't the central focus of your job, but merely incidental to work as a real lawyer.

Argument #4. Flexibility

Many solo and small-firm lawyers, especially those just starting out and working full-time, may put in nearly as many hours as their large-firm colleagues.

But solo practice allows you to set your own schedule, spreading out the work in a way that works best for you. For instance, suppose that your son or daughter has important after-school soccer matches that you don't want to miss. Back at BigLaw, you would probably be too embarrassed to cut out early more than once for a family event, and if you worked in government you'd have to use up personal leave. On your own, though, you can simply get an earlier start on your work day, or make up the time after the match when your kids are in bed. Sure, there will be days when you have a conference or a court hearing you can't postpone. But generally speaking, you have far more control over your own time when the law firm has your name on the door.

Moreover, when you run your own shop, you avoid many of the inefficiencies and superficialities endemic to any large employer: the practice group meetings, the sensitivity training sessions, the ceremonial lunches, and the office happy-hours that cut into the day without relieving you of deadlines or billable quotas. In addition, at large firms, face-time is paramount to success; simply being seen by your colleagues is just as important as actually getting the job done. So, if your assigned partner prefers to remain at the office until eight, you can count on staying until after eight most nights even if you'd rather arrive at dawn to get home by dinner. Then there are the non-billable demands.

Though most associates believe their salaries more than compensate for long hours at the office, the actual calculations prove otherwise. A well-known study by the Yale Law School Career Office shows that with various non-billable workday interruptions, an associate working a 60-hour week will bill only 42.5 hours, barely meeting a 2,000-hour minimum billable requirement. Spread over a 60-hour work week, (and assuming three weeks for vacation) that $160,000 salary amounts to roughly $55/hour, which doesn't seem so bad until you consider that it amounts to just 25 percent of a large firm associate's billing rate!

And for lawyers who want or need to work part-time, few if any other alternative work situations can match the flexibility of solo practice. Though lawyers choose part-time employment for many reasons, the most common reason is to enable lawyers to stay home with their children. For many years, law firms have been grappling— mostly unsuccessfully—with ways to accommodate new parents, primarily mothers, who want a part-time schedule. But at law firms, part-time often means working almost similar hours on less interesting projects at drastically reduced pay. Moreover, part-time frequently involves "work seepage", or at least an implicit understanding that a lawyer must drop everything when a case emergency comes up. As a result, some women don't take advantage of part-time programs even when firms make them available. You can't blame law firms or government organizations for not accommodating women any better. Not surprisingly, the partners give priority to their own financial well-being and the perceived needs of their clients over the desires of a handful of women asking for alternative schedules.

When you start your own firm, though, you're the boss...and your needs come first. You have complete freedom to design a schedule and a practice tailored to your specific family situation.

Argument #5. To Own Not Loan Your Talent

Lawyers toiling away at firms lose a substantial portion of their earnings to firm overhead and partner profit.

By way of example, a firm might bill a second-year associate at $250/hour, and collect $500,000 based on a 2,000-hour billable year. Of that, the associate receives only $160,000/year, or roughly a quarter of the firm's take. Granted, the remaining $340,000 isn't all firm profit; the firm covers your benefits (i.e., retirement contributions and health insurance), training and office space. But even deducting a generous $100,000/year for these expenses leaves the firm with a quarter-million dollars in profit. By contrast, if you were to start your own firm and generate 1,000 billable hours a year—that is, 20 hours a week at an average rate of $150/hour—you would still come out roughly the same as if you had stayed at the firm, but working far fewer hours! Just as we realize the advantages of owning rather than renting a home, lawyers should think carefully about the benefits of owning versus loaning their talents.

To be sure, solo practice has its ups and downs. After all, if you don't take care to adequately diversify your practice, or if you don't market your practice with vigilance, you could find yourself without any paying clients before too long. But consider: if you choose not to solo in these tumultuous times, you might be find yourself coping with a variety of grim scenarios: getting ejected from your law firm's partnership track after five years...getting unceremoniously booted from the law firm when you get too old...or, if you're working at a government agency, getting relegated to low-level cases when a new political appointee comes into power. What would you have to show for yourself then?

Argument #6. Opportunity to Innovate

Just as technology has transformed travel, publishing, and the media, so too, has it fundamentally altered the legal landscape.

As a legal futurist, Richard Susskind explains in *The End of Lawyers? Rethinking the Nature of Legal Services* (2010), that what he describes as disruptive technologies are automating many routine legal tasks, thus eroding the need for high-cost lawyers. Moreover, the Internet and cloud computing applications are enabling in-house counsel to bypass large firms and to seamlessly offshore their legal work (e.g., document review, due diligence and basic research) to India. As a result, many entry-level jobs at large law firms have been slashed by half, and they are unlikely to return. Law firm positions that do remain are being restructured. Firms are creating permanent staff attorney and non-partnership track positions to serve as a permanent source of leverage for entrenched equity partners. For details, read Steven Harper's article, *Permanent Leverage*; (AmLaw Daily, Nov. 12, 2010).

Nor are solo and small firms immune to change. Many solo and small firm lawyers who started practices 20 or 30 years ago still haven't quite made it into the Internet era. Even as today's consumers are accustomed to shopping and banking online, and spending considerable time engaged in online social media, *nearly half of solo and small firm practitioners lack even a rudimentary online presence* [ABA Technology Report 2009]. And still other traditional solo and small firms bemoan the rise of do-it-yourself providers like LegalZoom, which they believe are cutting into their business. Yet, they are unable to come up with viable models to compete.

These transitional times offer enormous opportunities for innovative, entrepreneurial lawyers to harness technology or to develop new business models for effective and profitable delivery of legal services. Large firms, with their multiple layers of bureaucracy, simply aren't nimble enough to run with new trends, while smaller firms have too much vested in the old ways of doing business to embrace change. Solo practice is an opportunity to innovate, and is a gateway for lawyers who have the vision to lead the profession into the future and change it for the better.

Argument #7. Career Satisfaction

More than any other career in law, solo practice offers great personal satisfaction. Several studies confirm that solo practitioners are more content than their large firm colleagues, noting that increased autonomy partly accounts for greater levels of satisfaction. So, too, does lower overhead and control over workload, which means that solos don't need to work as many hours. [www.abajournal.com/magazine/article/pulse_of_the_legal_profession]. Finally, most solos simply feel as if their work actually makes a difference. At a large firm or even at a government agency, lawyers are generally part of a team that collectively takes credit for victories. By contrast, a solo's victories are their own. Moreover, many solos get to see the fruits of their labor up close, whether it's the client who avoids conviction, or keeps custody of the kids, or the company secures an environmental permit or venture funding.

Doing work that matters is richly rewarding and makes solo practice a more meaningful—career-satisfying—experience.

BY CAROLYN ELEFANT, ESQ.
EXCERPT FROM SOLO BY CHOICE 2011/2012: HOW TO BE THE LAWYER YOU ALWAYS WANTED TO BE

CHAPTER 13

Finding Work Inside,
Outside & Around the Law

This chapter lays out the basic steps in any job search, from research and preparation to conducting the search itself. I will discuss some additional considerations if your plan is to be self-employed. I will also provide several exercises to create your list of transferable skills that will help in "packaging" yourself, and a master list of contacts for the purpose of networking. At the end of the chapter, you should have a concrete plan to begin your search for work that leads you to greater job satisfaction.

Successful career transitions don't just happen.

As I mentioned earlier, the process is usually longer and more complex than you imagined…especially if you wish to leave the law completely. And very often it's the ordinary external forces—finances, family, time, etc.—that require us to balance the ideal job against more practical considerations.

So, here's a reality check. Ask yourself…

- Are you fully committed to your goal of making a career transition?
- Do you have the support of your family, or any others directly impacted by your career change?
- Are you prepared to take a cut in pay that might be necessary to achieve job satisfaction?
- Are you prepared to devote time outside your other responsibilities to the demands of the job preparation and search process?
- If your family is not enthusiastic about—or are actively resisting—the prospect of change, can you count on their support in the future?
- If your ideal job requires a geographical move, are you (and your family) prepared to make that change?

These questions are not intended to discourage you. In fact, if you consider all the relevant factors at this stage—before making any final decision—you will be on firmer footing. And you will make an informed choice; a choice to which you can devote *all* your energy. On the other hand, you may not be able to answer all these questions right now. It only means that you may need to postpone your transition while you create a financial cushion, or until after your kids finish high school. Or maybe you need to scale back your hours or non-billable work to free up time for your job search. Or maybe you need to make a smaller change than you originally anticipated—either permanently, or as a short-term phase while you work out your long-term strategy.

> **Case study #1.** *Edward decided he wanted to become a human resources consultant. However, he had a lot of debt and no savings, and wasn't prepared to make a move right away. So, he continued working at his law firm job full-time while completing a year-long training and certification program in human resources. Once he was certified, Edward proposed—and negotiated—a part-time working arrangement with his law firm so he could have more time to develop his consulting business. It took Edward another year to build a financial cushion. Once he did, he quit his law firm job to focus on his consulting business full-time.*

EXERCISE #1. ADJUSTMENTS TO IDEAL JOB

What is your reality check telling you? Do you need to make any adjustments to your goal or job search strategy? What do you see as the biggest challenge to finding your ideal job?

_____

_____

_____

_____

Research

You have done an initial reality check and weighed your ideal job against the practical considerations. And you have identified possible adjustments you might need to make. Now you are ready to start the process of finding work.

First, you need to determine whether your desired new job will require additional training or education. Sometimes, this will be obvious, especially if you are transitioning to a new profession with its own set of educational or licensing requirements for practitioners. Or perhaps no further education is necessary, like when you are making a relatively small change within the legal profession. For changes that fall somewhere in between, it may not be clear whether some additional training would be needed or maybe just advantageous. Your research on this question should involve Internet searches about your desired field, as well as talking to individuals who already work in the field. See Appendix B for a list of legal and nonlegal certificate and credential-building programs.

Second, you need to research potential employers. Are you looking for a new firm, a new practice area, new setting, new geographic area, new industry, or new company? In this next exercise, I want you to identify all the potential employers that would fit the desired job from your mission statement and then do some research on those employers.

EXERCISE #2. IDENTIFYING AND RESEARCHING POTENTIAL EMPLOYERS

Create a list of employers for whom you could work in your ideal job. For example, your list might be every law firm with a specific practice area in your city, or every law school in your state, or every multinational company in a particular industry with offices in the country. Write the results in the spaces below.

My Potential Employers:

_____

_____

_____

_____

_____

_____

_____

In the second part of this exercise, do an online search for each potential employer on your list. Look for news articles or blog postings about the employers, and see if you can start to get a flavor of the employer's culture. What you are looking for is a sense of which potential employers would be a good fit with your career identity. You also want to determine whether you already have contacts who work for any of your potential employers.

Here's an example of how this works.

Case study #2. *Through online legal directories, Jennifer created a list of all the law firms with a securities law practice in her city. Then she searched her local newspaper online, and found stories mentioning each firm, their cases, the names of some of the partners, their clients, and so on. From her fact-gathering, Jennifer narrowed her search down to three firms that really stood out to her. She even discovered she had contacts at one of the firms. Eventually, she was able to get an offer from that firm through the support of her contacts. It was her thorough research that led to the discovery of connections.*

What do you notice about the results of your research? What did you find out about your potential employers? Do any of them in particular stand out to you? Can you get a sense of the culture of any of them? Do any look like they might be a good fit with your career identity? What about contacts? Do you know anyone—or know someone who knows someone—who works for any of them? Make note of your initial impressions.

_____

_____

_____

_____

_____

_____

_____

Preparing for the Job Search

Résumé and cover letter preparation is thoroughly addressed in many excellent reference works, so I won't cover that ground here. But regardless of which books or online sources you consult, always (repeat, always) get someone to read over and proofread your résumé and cover letters for syntax and typos. After spending so much time drafting and editing these documents, it's easy to be so close to your work product that you might not spot any errors. Of course, by themselves a résumé and cover letter aren't likely to get you an offer, but you can definitely sabotage your chances by submitting sloppy documents. If you belong to a job-search group, or know someone else who is looking for work, help each other out by reviewing each other's résumés and cover letters.

Packaging yourself. If you're looking for a non-law or a law-related job, your legal background may be a plus…but you may equally discover that it is *not* viewed favorably, and you may even be treated with discrimination or outright hostility. Outside of legal circles, being a lawyer is not the automatic asset it was decades ago. So, you need to be prepared for potential bias. An employer, for example, may have a low or unfavorable opinion of lawyers in general, and not even give you a chance. Or, an employer may assume that you are not really serious about working for his or her company, and that you will leave as soon as you find another law job. Make sure you read Chapter 14 to see the most frequent objections in greater detail, and how to position yourself favorably. In brief, the best thing to do under adverse circumstances is to emphasize your desire to leave the law and to enter the new field, and to make sure that your résumé and cover letter, your networking, and your conversations with potential employers, all reflect your new commitment.

One of the benefits of doing the exercises in this book is that they will help you explain to a potential employer how your thoughtful self-assessment has given you extraordinary clarity about your future career direction—and that your research has led you to this potential employer. And, as I mentioned earlier, obtaining additional training or certification also signals to employers that you are serious about your new career direction (note: see Appendix B for a list of legal and law-related certificate and credential-building programs).

Of course, in packaging yourself—particularly for a non-law job—you will also need to show employers how your legal background translates to the new field and how you will provide value to the employer. In other words, how does your previous experience qualify you to do the new job, and how will you be an asset to the employer? This requires you to identify the legal skills you have that transfer to the new job. It also requires you to put yourself into the shoes of the potential employer and ask yourself what—from their perspective—is the main advantage of hiring someone like you.

EXERCISE #3. IDENTIFYING YOUR TRANSFERABLE SKILLS

From law school to practicing law, lawyers develop numerous skills that could transfer to other fields and immediately provide value to an employer. However, not all of your transferable legal skills will be equally important in a new job. *Your task, in making a job or career transition, will be to identify which of the skills you have developed will be most valuable in your ideal job—and to focus on presenting those to your potential employers.* For example, if you identified your ideal job as **Lobbyist** or **Policy Advocate**, some of the most advantageous skills might be Persuade, Build Consensus, Establish Rapport, Network, Educate, Persist, Generate Enthusiasm, Resourcefulness, Summarize, and Balance Directness with Diplomacy. Or, if your ideal job is **Financial**

Planner, some valuable transferable skills might be Active Listening, Long-Range Planning, Advise/Counsel, Manage Money, Empirical Research, Create Solutions, Simplify Complexity, Monitor Details, Connect People to Resources, and Inspire Confidence.

For this next exercise, list five of your most valuable transferable skills, *keeping your ideal job in mind*. You may not yet have developed all the skills you will need in your ideal job, but you will undoubtedly be proficient in some of them. If you get stuck, re-read the table in Chapter 9. You will probably see some overlap between your motivated skills and the transferable skills that would prove valuable in your ideal job. Make note of them in the spaces below.

My Most Valuable Transferable Skills Are:

_____

_____

_____

_____

_____

Now think back over your educational and professional experiences for situations in which you used these skills. Prepare an example for each skill that you could share with a potential employer, either in a cover letter or in an interview. For instance, if you are looking for a situation in which you used persuasion effectively, look beyond the confines of brief writing. Did you persuade your firm to adopt a new policy or practice? Did you convince a committee of the wisdom of your viewpoint on a particular issue? Did you persuade fellow law students to get a well-known speaker to preside at your graduation ceremony? Get creative! This exercise should instill some confidence in you—and hopefully a potential employer—that even though you haven't held this particular job before, you can demonstrate that you have already developed many of its component skills.

Examples of Using Transferable Skills

_____

_____

_____

_____

_____

EXERCISE #4. CREATING A MASTER LIST OF CONTACTS

In this next exercise, you are going to create a master list of contacts. Not just your current professional circle, but everyone you know. You never know when the person who cuts your hair could be cutting the hair of someone who works for your next employer. Or maybe the person you hired to do spring cleaning in your house did spring cleaning for your next employer. You just never know who has a connection that you don't know about. You've got to broaden your circle because you're trying to be creative, and you're also trying to get a job outside your usual sphere. So you want to first look at your own network and see who you know who might know someone in your target industry or potential employers.

You probably already have one or more lists of contacts, either in a smartphone or tablet, in a personal and/or work email program, in a contact relationship management (CRM) program, or in various social media programs that you use for personal or professional purposes. Take all of your separate contact lists and create one master list. You may be able to export or download some or all of your lists to a single program or document. If not, then print out all your lists so that you have one master hard copy to work with.

Most lists average about 250 people, but yours may be shorter or longer. One of the reasons for doing the exercise is that it just might jog your memory about someone who might have a useful connection. It also puts you in the frame of mind to talk to your hairstylist and your car mechanic and the waiter at your favorite restaurant. It will get you to be a little bit more unconventional in your approach to networking, instead of limiting yourself to obvious logical connections, because you won't necessarily find your route to your next job through the logical path.

After reviewing your master hard copy, list all your contacts who might possibly have connections in your target industry or potential employers.

Contacts with Potential Connections:

1. _____
2. _____
3. _____
4. _____
5. _____
6. _____

If you don't immediately notice any connections to your potential employers or target industry—whether direct or indirect—don't get discouraged. Just the act of creating your master list can be an advantage. You may remember a connection later, or you may now have created the mind-set of looking for connections everywhere. You can see how this works through the example of considering buying a new car. If you are focused on a particular make or model, suddenly you notice them everywhere. It's not that there are suddenly more of them on the road. It's just that you weren't paying attention to them before. The same phenomenon can happen with shopping for a new job—if you are tuned into potential connections, you may suddenly find you have more than you previously thought.

Informational Interviews

Now that you have created your master list of contacts, it's time to get started setting up some informational interviews. Maybe you are very familiar with the people you identified as having connections to your potential employers or target industry—close friends, family, neighbors, etc. In those cases, it clearly makes more sense to have a casual conversation. But if your potential connections are less well-known to you, it may be more appropriate to set up an informational interview. It doesn't have to be formal—you might suggest a cup of coffee with a longtime colleague or a fellow college or law school alumni. However, if you don't have any direct connections to your potential employers or target industry, either personally or professionally, you will need to start with people you don't know. These individuals could be people mentioned in a news article or who serve on boards of directors in your target industry. In this case, it is helpful if you can also identify a former lawyer who now works in your desired field. In this next exercise, you will do just that.

EXERCISE #5. PROFILES OF LAWYERS IN TRANSITION OR FORMER LAWYERS

Some newspapers have a feature section in which they occasionally profile lawyers in transition or former lawyers. Some bar journals do the same. For example, Joe used to be a lawyer and now he runs a restaurant. Or Susan has an apparel company on the side of her solo practice. You can call up these individuals, tell them about your planned transition, and ask to meet with them. Offer to take them to coffee just to chat. Let them know you are interested in learning about their path and seeing that it can be done. If approached respectfully, most people are happy to give a half hour or so of their time to help someone else.

Do some research about lawyers in transition or former lawyers who work in your target industry, and write their names below.

Lawyers in Transition or Former Lawyers to Contact:

1. _____

2. _____

3. _____

4. _____

5. _____

At this point, you may be having some concerns about confidentiality. That is natural, and it's a valid concern that you must address. There is no way to completely mitigate the risk of your current employer finding out about your job search. But it should be somewhat reassuring that lawyers can and do network discreetly and change jobs all the time. You will need to trust your instincts and develop your own comfort level with disclosure.

When you have decided to make a change within the law—especially in your own city—that is the most confidential situation of all the job-change scenarios. If you are in a delicate position with your current employer and concerned about confidentiality, begin your networking with people you think you can trust. Explain the sensitive nature of your situation up front and ask them to keep it in confidence. Of course there are no guarantees that your job search won't inadvertently leak out to the wrong people. But if you let your fears decide for you, you might never make a move. Sometimes you have to take a leap of faith.

In certain situations, you might even decide to be honest with your employer about your intentions. The risk is that you'll get fired, but employers don't usually fire someone for being unhappy with the job. It's just not the normal employer response. If you're working there, it's usually because they need you. They likely would have let you go if they didn't need you. There is another possible outcome if you tell your employer that you are not happy and would like to make a transition. Your employer could be understanding and cooperative and might allow you some time to look for another job. In fact, it wouldn't be uncommon to find that your employer thought that you weren't really committed to the organization and was hoping to find an exit strategy. Your unhappiness is rarely as concealed as you think. Your disclosure of your plan would take the pressure off them and provide the avenue for an amicable parting of ways.

If you think that the honest approach might work for you, give it some careful thought first, and talk it over with someone close to you whom you trust to give you objective counsel. You should also become familiar with the laws in your own jurisdiction about the rights of employees and know what risks you take. Is yours an employment-at-will state and can you be fired for any reason or no reason at all? Or do you have more protections?

You never want to burn your bridges if you can avoid it. You never know when you will need the assistance of someone with whom you previously worked. So providing a reason for your desire to move on can be tricky. It's never wise to make up a bald-faced lie. If you tell the truth, you never have to remember what you said. But you can be selective and diplomatic in telling that truth. Usually, people's employment decisions are complex and there is more than one reason for a departure. You can pick the true part about why you're leaving that would be more palatable to your employer, and that's what most people do.

Working for Yourself

If your ideal job is to be self-employed, you may be wondering how all of this applies to you. Many of these considerations are still applicable—you still need to clarify your own career identity and criteria for long-term career satisfaction, do a reality check, research your target industry, identify your contacts, and network. For those who want to work for themselves—whether as a lawyer in solo practice, a legal consultant, or a web designer—the job search part of the process entails researching all the things you need to know about setting up your own business.

In addition to legal and accounting issues, you will have a number of choices to make, such as whether to work out of your home or get an office? Do you market yourself or do you hire somebody to feed business to you or have some other non-sales strategy for getting business? How do you position yourself? How specialized do you want to be in your chosen field? How do you identify the targets that you're going after in your chosen field? The research process to answer those questions is not at all unlike the process of finding an employer. And the networking process comes into play also. But instead of networking to find a job, you network to find individual jobs, contracts, or projects.

Before you embark on self-employment, however, you should consider another facet of owning your own business—that is, do you have the personality or inclination to be an entrepreneur? Let's say you want to be a consultant. You've done all of the self-assessment exercises and determined that this is the work you want to do and that it's a good fit for you. And you really think you'd like to do it on your own because you'd like the autonomy. That shouldn't be the end of your inquiry. Consider the following unique aspects of self-employment, and ask how you will handle each one:

Marketing. Will you be happy doing rainmaking? If the thought of marketing yourself and your business makes you cringe, you're going to do it in spurts because you have to, but it's going to be very draining because it goes against your personality. Ultimately, it's going to feel bad to you. Many people who aren't natural networkers find creative ways to make it more palatable, but those who are the most successful at their businesses are usually the same ones who enjoy the sales and marketing process.

Structure. Do you have the internal discipline to focus when you need to and meet deadlines without anyone looking over your shoulder or checking on the status of your work? Of course, you will probably have client or customer deadlines, but it will be up to you to create whatever supports or structures you need to make sure you fulfill on those deadlines.

Social connections. If you have a strong need for social interaction in your work, sitting in a home office by yourself all day may feel too isolating. Occasional phone contact probably won't be enough to satisfy your need for human interacton. Self-employed people have found various ways to connect with others—office share arrangements; in-person client meetings; professional or trade association meetings; and so on. But you will need to take the initiative. In any case, you will need to give some thought to this important issue.

Cyclical income. Working for yourself means no more steady paycheck. Some entrepreneurs find this aspect of self-employment challenging, particularly when starting out. Do you have the financial discipline to save money when cash flow is strong? Do you have reserves or other resources to get you through leaner times? How you handle this crucial piece of the puzzle could make the difference between success or failure of your business. If you are determined to strike out on your own, learn to handle money wisely so that it works for you and not against you.

Outsourcing. In the beginning, you might choose to wear all the different hats in your business to save on expenses. At some point, though, you may want to outsource some of the tasks, especially if you don't enjoy them or aren't efficient at them. If someone else can do your business-related tasks faster than you, it might be worth the cost—provided you use the time you free up to go out and get more business or do the work you have. The exercise below will help you distinguish between the business skills you have, the ones you want to develop, and those you'd like to have someone else perform.

Give these issues some serious reflection and consider whether you want to do your ideal job on your own as opposed to within an organization.

EXERCISE #6. IDENTIFYING BUSINESS SKILLS

You will save yourself much frustration if you consider up front all the necessary tasks of running a business—some of which you may not currently be skilled at or inclined to do. What are your strengths? What are your weaknesses? Which business skills might you already have? Which tasks of running a business do you have absolutely no desire to learn? Which of those are you prepared to pay someone else to do? Do you want to do your own clerical or secretarial work? Invoicing, collections, bill paying, travel arrangements, ordering supplies? Web design and maintenance? Social media marketing?

Skills I Already Have:

_____

_____

_____

_____

Skills I Am Willing to Learn:

_____

_____

_____

_____

_____

Skills I Would Like to Outsource:

_____

_____

_____

_____

_____

Just because you don't have any entrepreneurial experience, however, doesn't mean you won't be successful. Sometimes, your determination and faith in yourself will give you the motivation you need to get out of your comfort zone and do the things you need to do to be self-employed.

Case study #3. *Consider Nick. After doing the self-assessment exercises, he had an epiphany about what he wanted to do next. "I want to open a flower shop," he told me. "I don't like the negativity of law, and I think that working in a flower shop would be a very positive thing. Besides, I love helping people." Nick's decision wasn't especially analytical or left-brained; it was a very visceral decision. . . based in part on some of the exercises in this book. The trouble was that Nick didn't know anything about flowers, he didn't have retail experience or business training, and no one in his family had had a store. Asked what he thought would make him successful at running a flower shop, Nick put his hand on his stomach and said, "I just know it." Long story short: Nick did go out and start his flower shop.*

We have now covered the whole job search process, from the initial reality check to networking with contacts to find your new job. This chapter covers a lot of ground, and you may be overwhelmed at all the steps it takes to change jobs. Don't get discouraged! Yes, it takes research. Yes, it requires preparation. Yes, you will need to network. And if you plan to strike out on your own, you have some additional legwork in front of you. But if you break the process down into each discrete step, you will find it more manageable. And your ultimate reward will be a new and satisfying career. When you look back from that place, all your hard work will seem worth the effort!

CHAPTER 14

Putting Your Best Foot Forward

A few years ago, a Minnesota study of law school alums found that nearly half of those who chose nontraditional careers faced resistance and stereotypes from potential employers. For some, the objection stemmed from a prejudice against lawyers; for others it was simply the employer's inability to recognize the transferability of a lawyer's skills and background. Stereotypes about lawyers are an "easy roadblock for an interviewer to throw in the way of an applicant," says Ken, a lawyer-stockbroker. When Ken wanted to change from law to institutional equity sales, he formulated answers to many legal stereotypes. "It really doesn't matter what you say as long as it is plausible," he discovered. "All you have to do is be prepared to answer the stereotype questions."

Before we get into the most-often encountered objections to background and experience, consider these four job interview suggestions:

Most interviewers begin by asking about your vision of the ideal job and boss, and the reason for your current job search. After that, expect to be asked about any unique qualifications or experiences that distinguish you from other candidates. Then it's show time, and the four most-often asked questions are these:

> *What are your short-term/long-term goals?*
> *What are the best and worst aspects of your previous job?*
> *What do you know about our company?*
> *What would your former boss/colleagues say about you?*

And, expect some questioning about your legal background (and be sure you have some better reason for your job search than you aren't making enough money where you are now).

Suggestion #1. If you have contacts in this new field, ask them what stereotypes or objections someone with your background might encounter. Honestly evaluate whether those objections apply to you. If they do, find a way to turn them into advantages for your prospective employer. If the objections don't apply to you, be prepared to offer examples from your past. Prepare at least one story for every objection you anticipate. Then, weave into your conversation examples of things you have done that show you do not fit their stereotype. For instance, if your interviewer wonders about your ability to be a team player, you might say something like, "The best part of practicing law for me has been working as part of a team to close a large commercial transaction."

Suggestion #2. Don't conceal a truth, hoping the employer won't care. You may have learned how to hide your feelings in court, but it's harder to remain impassive in a job interview. Your anxiety triggered by a half-truth may reveal itself in your body language or voice quality, and be perceived as deception or dishonesty. Don't wait for the employer to bring up a subject. Instead, raise an objection yourself as soon as you feel you've developed some rapport. You needn't linger on it, though. Simply point out the situation, acknowledge that the employer may be concerned about it, and explain why it will not interfere with your ability to meet the demands of this job.

Suggestion #3. Turn an apparent vulnerability into a virtue. If you were fired from your last job, explain how you grew from the experience. It indicates your competence in dealing with adverse situations. Or a new graduate can point out that he or she is ready to be groomed into the type of lawyer the employer needs—and that you're willing to accept a lower salary to get the experience. The experienced lawyer can tout his or her ability to be profitable from the very first hour, pointing to the wisdom and maturity that come with age.

Now let's take a look at a dozen or so objections you can expect, and how you might handle them:

1. You have no directly relevant experience.
This is where transferable skills analysis will play a very big role in whether you get the job. Because if there's nothing on your résumé that leads an employer to believe you can do the job, you need to make a compelling oral argument about how your background has prepared you for the work. "When I was looking to change from law to institutional equity sales," says one

former lawyer, "I formulated answers to many legal stereotypes. For example, when someone mentioned that law school trained lawyers for litigation, not sales, I made the point that presenting a case in court really was a matter of presenting your facts or arguments in the most attractive, concise and forceful manner...exactly what a good salesperson should do."

The strongest point most lawyers can make is their ability to learn quickly. For example, you might say: *In the practice of law, I've worked under pressure to solve a wide variety of problems in many different industries and fields, and for diverse clientele. One of the reasons I've been able to perform this work is my ability to get up to speed rapidly in new areas. I'm certain that ability compensates for whatever I lack in actual experience.*

Sometimes, though, just dealing candidly with an employer's objection can get you the job. Soon after graduating from law school, Donna began helping her parents resolve employment law matters in the family business. After about a year, she applied to be a human rights advocate in city government. When the interviewing panel wondered about her lack of experience, she was frank: "You're right, I don't have a background in human rights," she said. "But the work I've done representing individual rights in the workforce, and doing employment law work, taught me how to advocate for people without power." One of the interviewers later told Donna that the hiring committee admired her honesty. When she was hired, she was simply told to "brush up" on the city's human rights statute before her first day of work.

2. We don't want a lawyer in this job.

According to a story in the New York Times, "*Lawyers trying to switch careers say they are often typecast as narrow-minded, confrontational and unimaginative.*"

Against such opposition, career consultants agree that your best strategy is to deal head-on with these stereotypes. One tactic is to take the high ground, explaining that you left the law because you just didn't have "the killer instinct." Or perhaps introduce a little self-deprecating humor before an interviewer has a chance to say, "We don't want to hire a lawyer because they're too argumentative and competitive." Another objection is that all lawyers are "glory-seekers"...they're not team players. This one will be a little tougher to overcome because lawyers are rewarded for achieving a high profile based on individual accomplishments. Think about it: How do lawyers get new clients or partnership slots? By being recognized for being exceptional in some way—winning the most cases, bringing in the most business, billing the most hours. In contrast, corporate accomplishments are owned by the division, the department, the team; not any one individual.

So, you will need to extinguish any doubts about your capacity to be a team player by describing your accomplishments with phrases like "contributed to," or "participated in" or "worked as part of a group."

In short, play up your team spirit.

You can also be more assertive. If you think the interviewer holds—but isn't voicing—some prejudices against lawyers, bring them up yourself and explain why they don't apply to you. One non-threatening way to bring up the subject is to acknowledge your awareness of lawyer stereotypes, and tell the interviewer that you've done a lot of thinking about how you would present yourself to fellow employees or potential clients to overcome their prejudices.

For example:

- Some might believe that with my law background I'm not a team player. My experience shows that not to be true. In my position as volunteer coordinator of the hospital fund-raising project, I managed a team of 20 volunteers. All but one of them worked with me on the project from start to finish, and we raised 20 percent more money than in any previous year.
- One of my frustrations practicing law was the tendency of my peers to find fault with ideas and then reject them before researching and developing them further. That's one of the main reasons I'd prefer to get into an idea business like public relations. I consider myself a good brainstormer and creative problem-solver. I want to generate and implement new possibilities, not strike them down before we've had a chance to explore them.
- I know that some employers regard lawyers in sales or other business environments as deal-breakers rather than deal-makers. One thing I prided myself in when I was practicing law was my ability to get people who seemed pretty far apart to agree on something reasonable for all of them. As an example, I was able to settle a real estate lawsuit that had been pending for seven years and involved 15 parties.

In the process of separating yourself from negative associations with lawyers, you don't want to go so far as to dismiss your legal background. You simply want to demonstrate how your legal background makes you a bonus employee (or as one career consultant puts it, a "two-in-one" employee). You'll be able to understand lawyers and the legal system, interpret legalities for the rest of the organization, and use your non-legal people and team skills to get the job done. In other words, you're a value-added employee; your legal knowledge will add another valuable dimension to the organization.

On the other hand, if any of these stereotypes do apply to you, don't argue that they don't. After all, if you're accused of being contentious and confrontational, you'll only prove the point! Instead, show how that characteristic only strengthens your credentials. For example, "Sometimes being confrontational is an advantage in a management position. You need to have the courage to deal with difficult people, to confront them and get the issues resolved. My legal training has taught me not to fear conflict and to tackle problems head on."

3. Why would a lawyer want a job outside the profession?

No matter how well you write cover letters and résumés; no matter how sincere your enthusiasm and commitment to a new endeavor, you must be fully prepared for the question: "Why do you want to leave the profession?" First, be flattered. The question suggests the interviewer holds you in high regard. After all, it is possible the interviewer wanted to be a lawyer and can't understand why anyone in your position would be dissatisfied. Many members of the general public regard law as a glamorous field they might have pursued if only they had the talent and persistence. To some, anyone who would leave the profession is suspect.

If you can't find a job practicing law, or if you haven't yet come to terms with leaving the legal profession, the question—Why do you want to leave?—will sting. In fact, you might be asking yourself the same question and wondering, "Am I a failure?" In which case, it may cause you to behave as though you have failed. One former lawyer was complimented by an interviewer for having a "very, very great" background. The lawyer's response was, "I do?" The interviewer replied, "Yes, but you still think there's something wrong with not wanting to practice law anymore." The lawyer hadn't mentioned her feelings, but her body language apparently signaled "failure."

Remember, people want to hire successes. So, present yourself as somebody who has made a conscious, well-considered decision to do what you're doing. It's easier to explain your new direction when you've taken the time for self-assessment. It's nearly impossible when you haven't. The point is to come up with your own heartfelt explanation for wanting to move toward the position under discussion...rather than fleeing from your current one. For example, one successful candidate for a position as assistant director of a law school career services office explained her motivation this way:

"I've been working with families in crisis as a matrimonial lawyer for three years; client contact has been the most enjoyable part of my work. Career services work appeals to me because I want to remain involved in a field where I'm in close contact with people in the midst of change. But I'd prefer to work in a cooperative, rather than adversarial, environment. I see myself as a lifelong learner, and would very much enjoy being with the law school."

4. You can't afford to take this job.

The subtext is similar to the previous objection: *"Why would someone as well-educated as you consider taking a job that pays so little money? Something must be wrong."* It could also be that the employer is worried you'll quit as soon as you find a job in law that pays better (a separate objection handled at the end of this section). Usually though, this objection surfaces when the employer assumes your salary demands will be excessive. Consider the case of Alison: she was a well-paid (but unhappy) third-year associate at a large law firm. She decided to seek work in university management, and—in anticipation of a huge pay cut—moved into an inexpensive apartment and paid off her credit cards. When a job opened up at a law school in her state, Alison promptly sent in her résumé. But the review committee assumed she wasn't aware of the huge pay cut, and discarded her résumé. Undaunted, Alison obtained an interview by contacting several employees of the law school, described to them the steps she'd taken, and assured them of her willingness to accept a substantial pay cut. She was hired. Within two years, Alison was promoted to assistant dean for alumni relations at double her associate's salary.

5. You're too young.

If you're under 30, you've got other stereotypes to confront, and you must be prepared to counter them with concrete examples of competence. Many employers complain about being burned by younger workers who failed to demonstrate sufficient commitment to the organization, or to follow rules of etiquette in dress or communication, or to give adequate notice of quitting. Your personal demeanor in a job interview will speak volumes. At the same time, you must be prepared with stories of projects you saw through to the end, of commendations you received for good attendance or performance, and other examples of how you've met the expectations of prior employers. You can also point out the advantages of your youth:

- Being as young as I am, I have the energy to devote to my work. I have no ties keeping me in the city and I'm willing to relocate and travel regularly.
- I'm aware that I don't have a lot of experience, but I'm willing to take on extra projects and do what needs to be done. With me, you'll be getting more than your money's worth.
- I'm not likely to make the mistake of thinking that I know something I don't.

6. You're too old.

This unspoken (and illegal) objection actually suggests a number of questions: will you work well with younger managers? Will your salary expectations be too high? How long will you stay with the organization before you retire? Do you have any illness or disability that would interfere with your performance? The American Association of Retired Persons suggests that you emphasize the positive attributes of your age, including your accumulated experience, maturity, judgment, perspective, increasing responsibility, and consistent achievement. You can also point to your stability. The Bureau of Labor Statistics estimates that only three percent of workers in their 50s change occupations in any given year, while 12 percent of those age 25 to 34 take the plunge, and the annual career change rate for all ages is around 10 percent. As a result, according to a national outplacement firm, corporations believe that younger workers will stay an average of three to five years, while those in their early 50s are likely to remain until at least age 65. Since low turnover generally translates into increased efficiency, the older worker recoups for the employer any losses resulting from a higher salary or a shorter period of employment before drawing retirement benefits.

You might also try some of these arguments:

- Because of my age and status, I don't have the "family versus work" conflicts of so many other applicants. I can stay at work as long as it takes to get the job done.
- I pride myself on my flexibility, and I'm a very quick study when new approaches are needed.
- I have enough life experience to know that no job is perfect 100 percent of the time; I've learned to appreciate the positive factors of each assignment.
- I'm a seasoned veteran. I won't require training or orientation; I can dive right in without supervision and make a contribution immediately (as opposed to a younger job seeker's untested potential). Therefore, I'm worth a somewhat higher salary.

7. You're overqualified.

Second-career lawyers, especially those who reached a high level of professional responsibility before enrolling in law school, must defer to those who will be your teachers, even if they have fewer "life credits" than you. One law career consultant says that second-career lawyers need to express their interest in, and willingness to be, a junior member of a team. Younger employers may expect someone with your experience to disrupt the balance of power. It's your job to make them comfortable that you won't.

8. You were fired from your last job.

Tell the truth about losing your job, but take the opportunity to demonstrate how you've grown from the experience. In an interview, honestly but briefly recount the reasons for your termination, taking responsibility for everything including a difficult boss. Explain why you will not repeat the same pattern in this job. For example, you now believe in deferring to your boss's expertise, or your personal problems have ended, or you've learned to ask for help when you don't have the experience or knowledge to handle something. Don't try to hide the truth, hoping that you won't be found out. Many employers want to know about your last employment, even if you don't list a reference. It's best to provide the name of a contact who will speak fairly of your work. Be aware, though, that sometimes the hiring personnel will sidestep your recommendation and contact an acquaintance of theirs to confirm your explanation. Anticipate the worst of what your former employer might say, accept responsibility for that evaluation, and explain what you learned from the experience.

9. Your résumé has a noticeable time gap.

If you've been unemployed for a long time, determine why and how it relates to this job application. Have you now broadened your job search after evaluating the transferability of your skills? Were you trying to move into a different field but realize now you're more suited to this area? If you've had an illness and are now completely recovered, "stress that your illness is not likely to recur and briefly speak of your doctor's encouragement to get back to work. If your health outlook isn't that rosy, bone up on the provisions of the Americans with Disabilities Act."

If, instead, you took a long, unpaid "sabbatical" to travel, raise children, or just recover from burnout, seek employers who understand and appreciate adventure, balance, or personal growth. Before applying, review the lessons you learned during your break. Then present that detour in its most positive light, turning it into a strong selling point. As an example, one young lawyer spent a small inheritance skiing and traveling in Europe during a two-year sabbatical from private practice. He later obtained a position in-house with a sports manufacturer by explaining how pleased he was that he'd taken time out when he was young enough to enjoy it, and how eager he now was to get back to work.

10. You're a woman.

You'd think by now that gender would be less of a hiring issue than it is. But women lawyers comprise only 19.5 percent of all partners and just 15 percent of equity partners. And while the Bureau of Labor Statistics show that the gap between the men and women's wages continues to narrow, full-time female workers still make only 81.6 percent of what their male counterparts earn.

Female applicants face one main prejudice: that they may be more committed to their personal lives than to their job (as evidenced by the probability that they may want time to have children and raise them). To overcome this subtle and always unexpressed prejudice against women, let the interviewer know that you have experience juggling multiple responsibilities. For example, you might have been a parent while going to law school or when you studied for the bar exam. You might have taken on a demanding volunteer project while handling a heavy caseload. Maybe you were the primary caregiver for someone close to you while also holding down a full-time job. The more examples you have of when you successfully balanced conflicting demands, the stronger your case will be.

11. You're a member of a minority group.

Your objective isn't to turn someone who's against you, or who believes in negative stereotypes, into an avid supporter. Your goal is to simply reduce that person's negativity sufficiently enough so that it doesn't hinder your career. Most of the prejudice you'll encounter will relate directly to the question of whether you'll be compatible with the organization. Demonstrate your conformity through your actions and past history. If you cannot show a fit, ask yourself whether you really want to join an organization where your daily work experience might be very uncomfortable. Either seek employers with a reputation for open-mindedness or a proven track record of diversity, or set out to be a paradigm-shifter or trailblazer. No matter what choice you make, you must show the employer not only that you can do the job, but that you will fit in.

12. You have a disability.

Don't hide your disability. Achieving a legal education and career with an impairment speaks well for you. Your disability may even give you an edge when applying to large private and public employers who want to demonstrate their commitment to a diverse workforce. But an attempt to cover up a disability could backfire. One hearing-impaired lawyer with excellent law school credentials wanted to keep her difficulties secret, fearing employers would see her impairment as interfering with her ability to do a good job.

In several interviews, she did not hear the questions posed and responded inappropriately. By failing to reveal her hearing loss, she conveyed exactly what she feared she would: the employers thought she was inattentive or unintelligent. The best approach is to be straightforward about your disability without asking for sympathy. Show through your accomplishments (and a couple of glowing recommendations) how capably you've met the challenges of your disability in other environments.

13. You'll quit as soon as you find a job in the law.

If it's true, play fair. Admit that you'll continue your search for legal employment and point out what you'll be able to contribute to their operation in the meantime. Also assure them that you'll provide whatever length of notice they require. But don't expect this argument to sell very well, except for temporary or project assignments.

These examples are only the most obvious objections; you may hear of or experience others. As effective as you are at countering all these objections, it does not mean you will overcome them or even that you will get hired. After all, the prejudice may be intractable and you may simply be competing with others who are more qualified for that job. But you will never get anywhere if you can't at least address the employer's concerns. If you seem to be running into the same objections repeatedly, you may need to get some educational, volunteer, or internship experience. Or, you might need to expand your job search to target different employers.

For various reasons, your background will be perceived as an asset by some, and a liability by others. Accept that this is a normal part of the job search process. Be prepared to put your best foot forward, but realize that, ultimately, you can't control how others view you. Just continue to focus on identifying and networking with potential employers that are a good fit with your career identity, and your persistence will eventually pay off.

CHAPTER 15

The Personal Obstacles to
Career Satisfaction

For lawyers, the path to career transition and satisfaction is filled with all sorts of obstacles and hurdles. Some of them are obvious; others less so because of limiting beliefs or personal blind spots. A few of the bigger obstacles are financial, family considerations, and age, and simply not wanting to give up the prestige of being a lawyer. I'll tackle each of the major obstacles.

Let's begin with the Big Kahuna—money. This is probably the #1 obstacle confronting lawyers who want to make a career change...but who haven't pulled the trigger yet.

Obstacle #1. I can't *afford* to leave the law.

The inertia that one must overcome to transition out of law is very high. In part, this is because lawyers, on average, are still among the highest-paid professionals in the country. A lawyer making a good salary will have a hard time making a comparable salary in another profession or business. In certain occupations, sales for example, you do have high income potential. But by and large, lawyers usually have to take a pay cut when they go into other fields because many of them are at the top of the financial food chain at the time they leave the law. Here are some of the financial objections to leaving:

- *I don't want to be a lawyer anymore, but I can't afford a cut in pay.* The lawyer in this situation seems to have only identified that he or she doesn't like being a lawyer, but hasn't pinpointed the source(s) of dissatisfaction. Nor has this individual done sufficient self-assessment to determine what about the job *really* doesn't fit his or her career identity. This individual would benefit by revisiting Chapter 2 (*Why This Book Was Written and for Whom*) and Chapter 5 (*Introducing the Lawyer Career*

*Satisfaction Model*ᴿᴹ)to begin the process of getting clear about their career identity, to assess the income potential of their ideal job, and to get a more nuanced understanding of the money issue.

- ***The job I really want doesn't pay enough.*** Some lawyers in transition cite financial constraints when they learn they will need to take a cut in income. Variations on this theme go something like this: "*I've locked in a certain lifestyle to match my current income, and I don't see how I can change it.*" Or, "*I don't have enough savings to be out of work for more than six weeks.*" Or, "*I'm the breadwinner in the family, and I don't want to have to put my spouse in that position.*" These objections are often based on the unrealistic expectation that you should be able to get a job that pays close to what you earn now. But in this economy and job market, it is more likely that a job change will require a pay cut, even if only temporarily. Think of it as a *transition cost.* You need to expect it, and to plan for it.

- ***If you're looking at financial issues in the abstract, your objection is premature.*** You haven't done the self-assessment, and you don't really know yet what the required trade-offs will be. If you have done a complete self-assessment, identified what you want to do next, and researched how much income you can expect to make in that new job—and you are *still* sure that you can't get by on less money—then you need to look at what you want, and the experience you're really looking for. What are the real criteria behind what you want? Is there another job that might meet those criteria? Or is there another way you can get those criteria met besides changing jobs? If the job you've identified (that pays less) is the only way to get the experience you want, then look at it this way: have you ever wanted something so much that you've been willing to sacrifice something else to get it? What was the difference? If you don't feel excited about this career possibility, then maybe you need to go back and reevaluate other possibilities. Because when people become excited about an option, the objections don't necessarily go away, but they diminish and seem less insurmountable.

Obstacle #2. I have family considerations.

- ***I don't want to disappoint my family.*** Whether you are referring to your family of origin or the family you've created as an adult, this obstacle is tricky. It would *seem* as though you're being considerate of others' feelings, but often this is just a smokescreen to avoid having to deal with a job change. First, figure out what you might be avoiding by hiding behind this reason. Then you can decide how to approach your family about a prospective transition, and what that would mean for the family. If the family you are concerned about will be directly affected by your decision, your transition will obviously be much easier if you get their buy-in. If they won't be affected, then their support would be nice, but in the end it's your life to live. Sometimes, the person you don't want to disappoint is…yourself!

- *My family depends on me for their standard of living*. This statement presents legitimate difficulties because there is undoubtedly some truth to it. Of course your family depends on you for their standard of living. No one can tell you that you should take your kids out of private school or sell the family home. Lifestyle adjustments are very personal, difficult types of decisions to make. Again, make sure this is really your true objection and doesn't really just obscure some fear related to job change. If your family's welfare really is the concern, think about what you feel obligated to provide them over and above the basic necessities of life. Why do you feel that way? Would your being happy at work provide any benefits for your family in a non-financial sense? Would you have more time or energy to spend with them? Would you be modeling your values for them?

Obstacle #3. I'm too old (or too qualified) to leave the law.

Maybe the new field you want to enter typically attracts younger workers, and you're afraid you won't be given a chance, or that you'll be told you're overqualified. This is a valid concern; age discrimination exists, and job seekers (lawyers and non-lawyers) beyond a certain age are often told they are *overqualified* for various positions. However, there are ways lawyers can market themselves to prospective employers. See the discussion in Chapter 13 on identifying transferable skills and packaging yourself in the best possible light. And Chapter 14 addresses how to handle numerous objections (age, over-qualification, etc.). Sometimes the best option for senior lawyers is to sidestep the conventional route and create a job (see Chapter 12 on solo practice, and the discussion in Chapter 13 on working for yourself). You could also become an *intrapreneur*; that is, by persuading an employer to create a position for you, or to hire you to fill a newly created position. The benefit here is that the employer doesn't have firm expectations yet about the job or the person who should fill it.

Obstacle #4. I don't want to waste my law degree.

Some lawyers who want to leave the law, or to go into a law-related field, don't do so out of concern that they will have *wasted* their JD. This is a fallacy; the time and money you spent on your legal education is a "sunk cost." It's already been made. And whether you stay in the law or not, those student loans aren't going away (unless, in some states, you work in a public interest legal position). Yes, you will have to figure out a way to repay your school debt (no small task). In that sense, money is a real factor in your decision. But don't tie yourself down to a career decision you made in the past. If things aren't working out, then staying in the law won't make things better. In fact, it just compounds the problem. Also, don't make the mistake of thinking that spending your professional life doing something other than practicing law is a waste of your legal education. No education is ever wasted. In fact, most of the jobs that lawyers transition to do benefit from the skills and knowledge that they bring to the table. So, you're not really abandoning your legal training; you're just using it differently. Some employers look for law grads for just that reason.

Obstacle #5. I don't want to give up the prestige of being a lawyer.

Lawyers often identify so strongly with their profession that they're sure they'll lose respect; if not self-respect then the respect of others. In my experience, that has not been the case. Non-lawyers have enormous respect for a legal education, and lawyers and non-lawyers alike are impressed by the courage it takes to do something new. In time, you may find yourself taking pride in your new endeavors and accomplishments that have nothing to do with the law. And consider this: the norms and expectations around careers have changed in the last decade or so. Nowadays, it is considered normal to change jobs, even careers, several times in a lifetime. Furthermore, people with dual degrees, perspectives, and backgrounds, are in greater demand because they bring more to the table. So, don't think you're giving up the prestige of being a lawyer; instead, you're *adding* to your prestige by growing into a new field or job.

Obstacle #6. There is nothing out there for me.

When lawyers tell me, "*There is nothing out there for me,*" they honestly believe their situation is special; that there can't possibly be a job out there that would be a good fit because of their complex set of values, needs, interests, and so on. Highlighting this obstacle suggests they have not yet begun the process of discovering their career identity or ideal job, or that they haven't begun researching potential employers. In either case, this is a transparent excuse to avoid the necessary due diligence. If you are truly dissatisfied with your current work situation, then falling back on this objection will get you nowhere. Consider this: sometimes the problem is in thinking that only one specific job will be satisfying. This myopic, or narrow thinking, can get you depressed, especially in a down economy. Instead, I recommend you look beyond the specific job title, and focus instead on the experience you want to have at work. This way, a whole range of possibilities might open up. One thing is sure, though: doing nothing because you are convinced there is nothing out there will only reinforce your sense of hopelessness. Doing nothing is not an option.

Obstacle #7. I don't have time to look for a new job.

This obstacle seems completely unassailable, because most lawyers are very busy. However, most everyone has some time that could be freed up for something as important as changing jobs or redirecting your career. If time seems to be getting away from you, keep a time log. For a week or more, capture every activity regardless how small or irrelevant…and be as diligent as though the time log were for your law practice. Some people say watching TV (or playing games or streaming videos on their iPad) is essential recreation. Fair enough, but a time log might make obvious how much more time they are spending than they realized. Reevaluate how you spend *your* down time. Think about how you can use your time more creatively to assist in your job search process. Again, doing nothing is not an option.

Personal Blind Spots

Everyone has them.

Blind spots stem from our personality or from our habits or from limited vision. We only see our part of the world; we don't know what we don't know. Blind spots can emerge at any stage of the career change process. They are a kind of filter that prevents you from seeing something that might be a good fit but you don't know it. Blind spots frequently pop up at the implementation phase, when action is called for. At this fragile stage, lawyers and others encounter all sorts of personal obstacles, many of which are limiting beliefs that serve to keep the person stuck in his or her current situation. I have covered some of the most common objections already, but the variations are unique to every person.

There is an easy way to find out about your own limiting beliefs or blind spots. Complete the following sentence:

If time and money were no object, I would...

_____

_____

_____

The reason I don't pursue that opportunity is... _____

_____

_____

_____

Have you ever had something bad happen in your life, only to later have something very good come of it? At the time, it seemed that nothing positive could ever come from the bad situation, but that's because you were only looking at it from one perspective. You may not have had all the information. And you certainly didn't know what would happen in the future.

> **Case study #1.** *Consider Melissa, a new associate. She was in a car accident that turned her life upside down for a year. She sustained minor brain trauma, with injury to the frontal lobe. She had to cut back to part-time work and experienced major difficulties in memory, concentration, and "global" organizational thinking, not to mention physical pain. Melissa thought she might never fully recover. Thankfully she did, and the insurance settlement allowed her to buy a house. A couple years later, she decided to quit her job and take a yearlong trip to Italy. She sold her house and used the equity to finance her trip. Melissa claims that her year abroad was the best thing that ever happened to her. Not only was it a wonderful geographic and cultural adventure, but also it was the beginning of a whole new outlook on life, which led to a new career. It wouldn't have been possible without the funds received due to her car accident. Talk about a silver lining! Does Melissa want to repeat that year of suffering now? Of course not, but she wouldn't change the past for anything.*

What about you? What previously difficult experiences have you survived that turned out to hold benefits unknown to you at the time? Can you see how whatever we are looking at is never the complete picture?

Let's take another example of a hugely limiting belief that some lawyers struggle with: "*I failed at being a lawyer.*" It all depends on how you look at it. Something good usually comes out of what you might otherwise look at as a "failure." The story goes that a colleague of Thomas Edison once told him that several thousand of their experiments had been failures. The inventor's reply: *"Failures? Not at all. We've learned several thousand things that won't work."* If you only have two categories, success and failure, it's going to be pretty hard to recast everything as a success. Why not reframe your "failures" as educational experiences, learning curves, adventures, or personal growth?

Begin to train your mind to see things "in a different light," even if you receive no new information about the situation right now. Often, the "new information" will only come at a much later date.

It's often challenging to reframe situations ourselves. The best way to overcome blind spots is to be open to feedback from someone else. You might need a spouse, partner, friend, coach, or counselor to reflect back to you what they see. Find someone who knows you well to work through this process with you or hire a professional to help you. Sometimes, what seem like hurdles in the job change process are actually a lack of clarity, rather than true obstacles in executing a plan of change. You might need more information. You might need help in figuring out other possibilities. You might need a plan to test out the waters. Trying to do this alone can be very challenging. That's why it helps to have someone else to think through the issues with you.

Our Limiting Beliefs and Habits

What is the difference between the people who make a transition and the people who just can't seem to make the change despite being very unhappy in their current job? What makes some people more likely to make the jump?

The mind-set. Some people approach the career change process with hard-luck stories; stories about their lack of success or why a change in careers just wouldn't work for them. Or they'll say that they are considering changing jobs…but only at the urging of a spouse or significant other. Well, research shows that our mind-set has a significant impact on our success. Psychologist Martin Seligman (author of *Learned Optimism* and *Authentic Happiness*), has researched the differences between optimists and pessimists. Optimists are those who interpret events and circumstances that happen to them in a positive way; other the hand, pessimists tend to put a negative spin on events and circumstances (although they usually tend to describe themselves as realists). In Seligman's study, he found a range of benefits associated with optimism: optimists live longer, are healthier, have happier marriages, make more money, cope with change better, and so on. An optimist sees the silver lining. Fortunately, says Seligman, optimism is a learned behavior.

Risk aversion. Another reason some people make job changes and others don't has to do with risk aversion. Not surprisingly, lawyers as a group tend to be quite risk-averse. Much of the practice of law involves advising clients of the risks of a particular course of action—whether a lawsuit or a business deal—and how to limit their risk exposure. With so much focus spent on risk-avoidance in their jobs, it should come as no shock that lawyers would try to minimize it in their personal lives as well. The law encourages this mind-set and attracts people who are comfortable with it. This only becomes a problem when you decide you are unhappy and want to make a change, but can't bring yourself to leave the security of the familiar. On the one hand, it makes perfect sense: after all, why would you take a leap out into the unknown when there are no guarantees that all will turn out okay? On the other hand, does it make sense to stay in a job where you are unhappy? If you apply legal logic to a career-change decision, you may very well talk yourself out of doing anything. The desire to find a satisfying job is rooted in emotion, not logic; and emotions are a realm of human experience that many lawyers are uncomfortable with. But it may come down to this: Are you willing to put logic aside and take a risk for the sake of your professional happiness? Are you willing to take the risk of *not* changing?

Inertia. I mentioned before, when discussing money hurdles, that inertia keeps many would-be job changers anchored in their unhappy positions. If you don't have a job and need one right away, then this won't apply to you. Immediate financial survival and paying your bills is all the incentive you need. But if you have a job and nothing requires you to leave, it can be surprisingly challenging to make any kind of change, even if you know what you want. It's truly as though this law of physics keeps us chained to the chair in our office. To make a successful transition, you will need to overcome this gravitational force—by taking consistent action. Any small action will do to get you started. Continue with small action steps. Every day, do at least one thing toward your desired new job:

Do one self-assessment exercise.
Research a prospective employer.
Revise your résumé.
Prepare a cover letter.
Join a job search support group.
Contact someone to ask for an informational interview.
Attend a networking event.

Write a thank-you note.

Make a follow-up call.

Reach out to a friend for support.

Do whatever you need to do to get going, but just do something—every day. After awhile, the actions begin to build on each other, and you create some momentum. To sustain the momentum, keep taking small, consistent action.

Don't Worry if Your First Job Isn't the Right One

Some people do all the self-assessment work and still are not able to match their career identity to an ideal job. They don't have a calling, and they still don't know what to do with their lives. They worry whether any job they choose will be the "right" job for them. Even many people who can identify an ideal job worry whether it will be the "right" job. Just assume from the start that it won't be the "right" job, that is, it won't be where you end up. The first job you get transitioning out of law is likely going to be the "wrong" job in that it's not your ultimate destination. Stop thinking about "right" and "wrong" jobs and just select the best alternative right now. You are going to do what sailboats do—it's called tacking. You zigzag across the lake to capture the wind and get where you're going. By going from one job to another, and building on what you learn along the way, you often evolve into the position where you will ultimately land—and it's often not where you envisioned yourself being at the outset of your journey.

CHAPTER 16

Should I Leave the Law?

In moments of reflection, many practitioners admit that one of their main reasons for attending law school was for the external rewards—money, prestige, respect, security. Later, if they decide to leave the profession, they talk about the difficulty of giving up their lawyer identity. For some, this change is especially disorienting ...

"It was tough going in every morning to practice law. I used to wake up and think, 'Maybe they'll declare World War III, and I won't have to go into the office.'"

"When I practiced, one of the most self-defeating things I did was believing that there was something wrong with me for not liking my work. I had this perception that everybody else in my firm was doing quite well, and that they all loved their work. I'd look at them and wonder, 'How is it that you like it?', and try to figure out what was wrong with me. I thought that if I just fixed me, I could be like them and enjoy the law."

"One night I dreamed that I won the lottery, and all I could think of was, 'I'm free, I can quit my job!' When I woke up and realized it was only a dream and I was still trapped, I was so depressed that I couldn't go into work that day. I did eventually leave [my firm], but it took me a couple more years to finally cut the cord."

"There's a stigma to changing careers after practicing law," says Wendy, a former lawyer. "Believe it or not, it is more acceptable to change firms many times, or to hang out your own shingle, than to leave the practice of law."

So, maybe you're worried that if you admit to being tempted to leave the law that you'll invite an onslaught of negative comments...or that your family and colleagues will see you as a failure. According to one survey of

Midwest law graduates working in nontraditional environments, the most common personal obstacle in the transition process was opposition from friends, family and colleagues. This barrier was bigger than the grads' own anxiety, the loss of prestige, the feelings of shame or failure, and even their worries about financial sacrifice.

Michael tells the story of leaving the law to become executive director of one of the largest nonprofit organizations in his region of the country. Walking downtown one day, he bumped into some of his old law buddies. *"Before I could even say what I was doing,"* says Michael, *"My friends all lowered their eyes out of embarrassment for me. After all, I used to be a partner in an A-rated law firm. What happened to me?"*

Doug, who also left the law—to manage marketing at a major sports equipment company—also remembers the confusion his decision created among some of his colleagues:

> *"The first month after I announced I was leaving, other lawyers would meet me on the street and say, 'You can't leave.' I'd say, 'Why can't I?' And they'd say, 'Well, you've got a great practice.' And my response was always, 'Yeah, but I don't like it.' So, they would look down at their shoes and just walk away. But after I started working at my new job, I began getting calls from these same guys. They'd say things like, 'I'm really kind of dissatisfied with private practice, but I can't seem to pull the plug. Could I come out and talk to you?'"*

No matter what your professional status, your choice to trade your lawyer identity for a different one will trigger a period of emotional ups and downs. Consider this lawyer's experience:

> *"I practiced general civil law for nearly 15 years, the last 10 of which I solo'ed. I maintained a diverse clientele and rendered services in nearly every discipline of law. Despite the variety of my career experiences, I had no passion for my work. About a year ago, I simply burned out and quit my practice without any career plans. My business telephone line and stationery are my only remaining ties to the legal profession. The past year has been filled with near-equal doses of doubt, anxiety, frustration and self-discovery. Reading about others who have dropped out of law has been a newfound source of reassurance and inspiration and, in that regard, has provided much needed relief to my understanding spouse. Only recently have I begun my search in earnest for a new career."*

Breaking ties to the profession leaves you without a sense of belonging. And that's one very uncomfortable state of being. The good news is that once you start the process of moving closer to finding satisfaction, you will eventually feel better. On the other hand, if your fear of the future keeps you stuck, you'll be doomed to be in the doldrums for a lot longer. *"Before you make a break,"* says one former practicing lawyer, *"you have to overcome your own ego. My ego was right there in front of me all the time. It said, 'I'm a lawyer', and I kept running into it."*

How can you break through this daunting barrier? The most important ingredient is support, and reaching out to others who have already made the change or who themselves are struggling through the same process. I will talk more about the importance of a support system in Chapter 18.

CHAPTER 17

The Disengagement Process

Editor's Note: If you have decided to stay in the law, and change firms or start your own solo practice, some special considerations apply to your departure. For example, how do you negotiate benefits…When can you tell your clients…What are you allowed to take with you? This chapter, an excerpt from Carolyn Elefant's *Solo by Choice 2011/2012*, guides you through this minefield of potential ethical violations, so you can start your next job with a clean slate and a clear conscience. If you have decided to leave the profession, whether for a law-related or non-law job, you'll need to know how to close an active practice and cover yourself for any future malpractice claims. The end of the chapter contains a brief discussion on steps to take if you are leaving the law.

Before you can make a fresh start, you need to sever ties with your existing employer. Whether that departure is involuntary or voluntary, emotions and self-interest often contaminate the disengagement process.

When you disengage from your firm, you walk a thin line between protecting your rights and taking the high road. Of course, you should vigorously negotiate for what you're entitled to, whether it's a fair severance package if you've been terminated, or an assurance that the firm will promptly transfer files for clients who choose to follow you to your new practice. Whatever the circumstances, avoid lawsuits, and badmouthing your firm, and skulking out with a pile of client files in the dead of night. Even in large metropolitan markets, the legal community is a much smaller place than you can imagine. In the long run, burning bridges or otherwise acting unprofessionally will cost you many future opportunities.

In this chapter, I discuss issues relative to disengaging from your firm, including involuntary departure (e.g., giving notice, negotiating benefits), voluntary departure, and the divisions of clients and assets.

Disengaging From Your Firm

Involuntary departure. How you give notice depends primarily on whether your departure is voluntary or forced. Obviously, when the firm lets you go, your own notice is not as important since the firm already knows you're leaving. Under these circumstances, the only decisions you have are whether—and when—to announce that you are starting your own firm. During your final weeks, you should definitely mention the possibility of starting a firm as one of your options. If colleagues know you're thinking about solo practice, they may have ideas about other lawyers with whom you might speak; they may even have potential referrals. Many times, firms—or at least individual partners or associates—feel badly or guilty about an economic-induced lay-off, and will try to help you with possible leads. Firms sometimes even make office space available on a temporary basis to a terminated lawyer who wants to start a firm. Even though you've been fired, assess the situation carefully. Don't make your plans for going solo sound too definite if you believe the firm may try to limit your access to client files, or worse, that they may contact your clients and tell them you've been let go to prevent those clients from following you.

Voluntary departure. In many ways, departing a firm voluntarily is more difficult than if you'd been fired. Sure, you don't experience the same powerlessness and embarrassment as when you're told to leave. On the other hand, you still need to deal with colleagues who may feel betrayed by your departure, or who view your motives with suspicion, believing you want to steal clients or bring down the firm. Below are some do's and don'ts about disengaging. Note: leaving a government agency or in-house position is not as complicated because you don't have to address the issue of dividing clients or money, which is always the sticking point when lawyers leave a firm. At the same time, some recommendations (such as always act professionally), apply no matter what position you leave:

Learn from others. Before you give notice, investigate how your firm handled lawyers who left the in the past, and consult with a lawyer who has already left the firm. If that's not an option, make discrete inquiries about the firm's practices.

Consider the following questions:

- *How has the firm treated departing lawyers in the past?* Did it deal fairly, giving a reasonable time to clear out their offices, and to copy their work product off the computer? Or did the firm have the departing lawyer escorted from the office soon after the announcement?

- *How did the firm provide notice of a lawyer's departure to existing clients?* Did it send a joint letter with the lawyer, or did the managing partner get on the phone to alert clients and discourage them from leaving the firm?
- *How has the firm handled transition of clients who decide to follow the departing lawyer?* Did it cooperate in transferring files for clients who followed a departing lawyer to a new firm, or did it insist on retaining files in the hopes of deterring clients from moving to your firm?
- *Has the firm had a negative experience with a departing lawyer* (i.e., someone who stole files and solicited clients even before he or she was out the door)?

Be prepared. It doesn't hurt to prepare for a worst-case scenario in which your firm sends you packing on the same day you give notice. In this situation, the firm would close ranks, and deny you access to your computer and files by deactivating your security codes and password. Of course, this means you would lose the ability to save what's rightfully yours. So, before you give notice, save copies of all of your work product and e-mail messages; any client materials you're entitled to retain; and start bringing home the seminar materials, bar journals, and other publications that belong to you. As I will discuss later, you must *absolutely positively* refrain from soliciting any clients while you remain part of the firm. But do have a pre-drafted e-mail announcing your departure to clients. So, if the firm does cut you loose upon giving notice, you can preempt the firm's announcement with one of your own. Note: some bars prohibit departing lawyers from contacting firm clients without authorization from the firm.

Have consideration. Give your firm the traditional two weeks notice… if not more! And, when possible, avoid giving notice in the weeks before a major trial or closing. Assure your firm that you will remain around long enough to finish outstanding work, or to brief a new lawyer on the matter. Of course, your firm might decline your offer; in fact, they might ask you to leave right away. But at least you can be satisfied at having acted professionally. This end-game can also end on an up-note: a colleague once told me that when he left his large firm, he wound up continuing to handle work for his employer for six months after his departure on a contract basis, which helped ease him into solo practice.

Act professionally. Resist the temptation to sneak into the office to collect client files, or to drop a letter of resignation on the managing partner's desk. Such conduct forecloses any future referral opportunities from your firm…not to mention the bad feeling it leaves with colleagues. I've spoken with several lawyers who were left in the lurch by departing associates who sneaked out with law firm files. Years later, these colleagues *still* refuse to refer clients to those former associates. Of course, if you do stoop to such conduct, lost referrals would be the least of your worries. Under the ethics rules of almost any jurisdiction, taking client files would invite a civil lawsuit or bar complaint by your former firm. Do you really want to spend your first few weeks or months of practice defending yourself against your former firm before a disciplinary committee? And put yourself in your employer's shoes; after all, someday, you may be in a position where some of your associates leave your firm to hang out their own shingle. How would you feel if they left you with imminent deadlines and no information about outstanding cases? So, leave your firm with the same professionalism and grace you'd expect from your own employees.

Before You Leave: Negotiating Benefits

When you leave your employer, you may be entitled to certain benefits, such as compensation for vacation time or the right to purchase health insurance through COBRA. But in contrast to when you started your job and HR took care of all of these matters for you, it's up to you to ensure that you receive all rightful benefits before you leave. Negotiate vigorously for what you deserve; every little extra bit of cash can help alleviate the financial stress of the early days of starting your own practice.

Benefits you want to actively negotiate

Vacation/sick days. Many lawyers leaving a firm or the government find themselves with three or four weeks of unused vacation. Check with HR or your employee manual to determine whether your firm is required to pay for remaining vacation and sick days. Even if the firm maintains that it is not obligated, its position may be at odds with the labor laws in your state. Why bother? Because the compensation you receive for unused time can amount to the equivalent of almost another month of salary, a big help if you're starting out without a source of revenue.

Retirement contribution and bonuses. In contrast to vacation benefits, which accrue all year long, some benefits—like retirement contributions or bonuses—are distributed annually, usually in January or February for the previous year. If you're leaving voluntarily, you may be able to time your departure so that you're around when these benefits are dispensed. However, if you're asked to leave late in the year, you may miss out on these benefits unless you speak up. Again, consult your employee handbook and

HR manual. If you've already met the criterion for a pension contribution or bonus, then make your case for receiving it.

COBRA. Federal law requires employers with 20 or more employees to provide employees and their dependents the right to continue health insurance coverage for up to 18 months after leaving a job. Even though COBRA requires you to reimburse your employer for its share of your insurance premiums, COBRA coverage is generally lower than what you could get on your own since you can take advantage of your employer's group rates. COBRA imposes strict deadlines for electing coverage so it's up to you to stay on top of the process to avoid missing a deadline.

Unemployment. If your separation is involuntary, you probably qualify for unemployment benefits. Don't be ashamed or proud to take unemployment; after all, you've been paying into the system for as long as you've been working. So, you might as well take what you've earned. Some states allow unemployment so long as you certify that you are continuing to seek employment, something you can truthfully claim even after starting your firm (for example, it's likely that you might apply for contract work positions after you start a firm, which constitutes looking for other work). In addition, you must report any earnings you receive from new jobs so that you do not exceed the maximum level of employment that you're entitled to by law. After what you've been earning at your firm, unemployment doesn't amount to much; maybe $300 to $400/week for a finite period. Still, that may be enough to cover some bills while your practice gets off the ground. Note: some states do not permit the self-employed to collect unemployment.

Other benefits. Believe it or not, even if you've been terminated from your position, you have some leverage in negotiating benefits. If your firm fears you might bring a lawsuit, it may try to avoid the possibility by placating you. Or one or more of the partners may feel so guilty about your dismissal that they will try to ease their conscience by giving you what you ask. Example: if you've been told to leave by May and the firm pays bar dues and other licensing fees in June, ask that they pay these costs for the year. If you're forced out in the last quarter of the year, maybe the firm will pick up the tab for health insurance premiums through the end of the year. This would be especially helpful if you intend to switch over to your spouse's plan, and you're not sure how long that process will take or whether you need to wait until the end of the year to put it in place.

Are They Really Your Clients?

Don't be surprised at how hard your firm fights to keep clients, even clients you brought to the firm yourself, or clients who originated with the firm but where you acted as managing lawyer. Nor is it hard to understand why…even in the case of a client whose matters you handled exclusively, or who only generated several thousand dollars in business. Clients are the firm's most important asset…for more reasons than money. Their retainers and fees serve as a law firm's sole source of revenue, providing the high six-figure incomes, the box seats at sports games, the expense-account dinners, the designer office interiors. Even prominent clients with smaller matters bring prestige to the firm, enabling it to capture future business and ensure future growth. Thus, firms worry that news of a loss of even a few insignificant clients to, of all people, a lawyer going solo, might damage the firm's carefully cultivated reputation.

Ethics rules. As much as firms may want to keep clients, ethics rules impose some limitations that can level the playing field…at least a little.

In contrast to private corporations, law firms can't execute non-compete agreements to prohibit former lawyers from soliciting existing clients. Both the ABA Model Rules of Professional Responsibility, and every state bar, take the position that clients have an unfettered right to choose their lawyer. And any practice which restricts a client's ability to choose—whether it's a non-compete agreement, or a law firm's ban on communications between a former lawyer and firm clients, or a firm's refusal to turn over client files so that a client can transfer to another lawyer—will not pass muster under ethics rules.

Still, law firms have some wiggle room.

Ethics rules don't stop a firm from offering an existing client all kinds of perks to remain with the firm.

In fact, ABA Opinion 06-444 held that a firm can ethically make retirement benefits contingent upon a lawyer's agreement to sign a non-compete clause (source: ABA Journal e-Report, May 25, 2007; www.abanet.org/journal/ereport/my25ethic2.html). Furthermore, ethics rules don't prohibit a firm from highlighting the disadvantages of being represented by a solo practitioner rather than the law firm whose very letterhead causes opponents to quake in their boots. In addition, the rules impose limitations on departing lawyers. Both the ABA rules and most state ethics codes forbid lawyers, while still employed at their firm, from soliciting firm clients with whom they do not have a personal, working relationship. Some state codes go further, banning solicitation attempts between firm lawyers and all clients, even where a personal lawyer-client relationship exists. Law firm employment or partnership agreements may also prohibit pre-departure solicitation of clients, even if ethics rules don't.

Then there are, in the words of Dennis Kennedy, author of *Leaving a Firm: Guidelines to a Smoother Transition,* "the petty little games" that some law firms play.

For example, one firm's refusal to turn over client e-mails on the grounds that they did not comprise part of the client file...or the firm that required departing lawyers to pay exorbitant rates to have client files copied so that they could retain the copies after transferring the files...or the firm that argued they were entitled to fees for the entire client matter even where the client moves to another firm in the interim! All such behavior interferes with the client's ability to remain with the departing lawyer. But don't expect to see any of the rules clarified in a way that benefits the departing lawyer. As long as the ABA and the state bars are dominated by large firm interests, any attempt to close these ethical gaps will be resolved in favor of the large firms.

Soliciting and Dealing With the Firm's Clients

DO refrain from actively soliciting existing clients while still employed at the firm. As previously mentioned, bar rules aren't completely clear on whether lawyers still employed at the firm can solicit existing clients with whom they have a personal relationship. Ethics rules generally preclude solicitation of clients where there's no personal relationship. But just to be safe, refrain from actively soliciting firm clients while you're still employed at the firm. The line between solicitation and ordinary small talk is awfully thin, though. ABA Rules and most codes define a solicitation as any kind of communication, motivated by pecuniary gain, concerning a lawyer's availability for employment. So, telling the client you're leaving to start a firm and asking him or her to come with you constitutes an impermissible solicitation. But floating the idea that you might want to start a firm probably is not (though here, you want to be careful that word doesn't get back to your firm, which might send you packing sooner than you imagined). If a client said to you that she wished you practiced at another firm because your firm's fees are too expensive, it would be appropriate to say, "I'll give that some thought." But sending her a brochure and a proposed retainer agreement probably is not. Beyond ethics rules, use common sense and courtesy. At the end of the day, it's not worth putting your firm on the defensive for clients that may come with you anyway.

DO have an ethically compliant letter to clients ready upon giving notice. When you give notice of your departure, you should already have drafted a letter informing clients of your departure, and advising them of their right to remain with the firm or to come with you. Since your firm will probably want to notify clients themselves, having your own letter or e-mail already drafted gives you a chance to pre-empt the firm's announcement. Keep in mind that some jurisdictions may prohibit you from contacting former firm clients unless you transmit notice jointly with the firm, or if the firm pre-approves your announcement. Some rules may also restrict you from contacting clients with whom you did not have a personal relationship. Check your state ethics rules on departing lawyers, and consult with bar counsel before you send anything to existing firm clients.

DO settle unpaid balances for existing clients before you leave. The clients who follow you may have a variety of different billing arrangements with your existing firm. Some may owe outstanding balances for work that has already been completed; others may pay a flat, monthly retainer under an annual contract. If you're a partner in the firm, the partnership agreement probably provides for the percentage of disbursements to which you're entitled from clients, as well as a provision for resolving division of profits when a partner departs with a client. Here, you need to determine whether it's worth it to fight for every last nickel, or simply to cut a fair deal and get on with your life. As an associate, your rights to fees from existing clients may be more limited since you were paid a set salary rather than a share of profits. So, if you take several contingency matters with you where the firm fronted significant costs, you (or your client) will have to compensate the firm for its investment in the case after you receive a judgment just as any other client would who switches lawyers midway through a contingency proceeding.

DON'T even think about swiping office supplies. You may think that you're saving yourself money by taking legal pads, pens or other office supplies from the firm before you leave. And the temptation to copy software licensed to the firm is probably even greater. In fact, if you've been fired, you may feel justified as compensation for unjust treatment. But the cost of office supplies is negligible, and if you poach licensed software you don't have access to the help desk or upgrades. It's just not worth it. Anyway, why lock yourself in to your firm's way of doing things? Make a fresh start. Your firm isn't likely to catch you sneaking supplies, but think how foolish you would appear if they did. What argument could you make? That you can't afford to buy software now that you're out of a job? Not the sort of impression you want to leave on a firm that you hope will send you referral business.

DON'T use firm resources to solicit clients. One lawyer learned the hard way that you shouldn't use firm resources to solicit clients. He used firm letterhead to solicit clients under the guise of being employed at the firm, then took the cases and handled them on his own. Use of firm resources isn't limited to stationery, however. Most firms maintain detailed databases of clients, including client contacts and background information. That data belongs to the firm, which means you cannot take it and use the information to contact clients after you leave the firm.

DON'T steal client files, but DO keep copies. When you leave your firm, do not, under any circumstances, leave with client files whether you worked on those matters or not. Under ethics rules, client files are considered property of the client and held in trust by the firm. Taking files without permission is stealing, and that can expose you to ethical sanctions. If you're discovered taking files, don't expect your former firm to go easy on you, even where the client was likely to follow you anyway. Firms need to retain client files for malpractice purposes. By taking client files, you compromise your firm's ability to defend itself in future malpractice actions, creating problems for the firm with its insurance carrier. All of this would make your firm angry enough to file ethics charges against you...and the firm would probably prevail. At the same time, you should retain copies of client files, or at least key documents from those files, for matters in which you were personally involved. State ethics codes do not address the issue of copies, but copying files would probably pass muster as it does not compromise either the firm's or the client's ability to access the original files. More importantly, departing lawyers must keep file copies as a matter of self-preservation. Should malpractice claims arise in the future, a lawyer must have proof where his involvement in the case terminated so that the firm does not attempt to transfer the blame for malpractice.

DON'T badmouth the firm to get clients. After you leave the firm, you may be tempted to convince one of the former clients to come with you by sharing some not-so-flattering information about your former firm. The information might be general in nature, (e.g., a law firm policy that allows the firm to double-bill hours spent in travel to Client 1 and work done during that time to Client 2), or information that is specific to the client (e.g., the managing partner calls the client an annoying dweeb). Don't do it. Badmouthing can potentially expose you to a defamation action; also, it makes you look infantile and unprofessional. Further, it's not an effective marketing technique. Criticizing your old firm may give your client a reason to leave, but it won't give the client reasons to come with you.

TAKING CLIENTS WITH YOU: EXPECTATION VS. REALITY

As you plan your departure from your firm, be realistic about which clients are likely to follow you. Obviously, you can't expect Corporation X, a 15-year client whose CEO is a close, personal friend of the managing partner, to jump ship. Especially when you've only handled his company's matters for three years and dealt with contacts as junior as yourself. At the same time, other more likely clients may also decline to come to your firm for one or more of the reasons outlined here by lawyer/author Dennis Kennedy:

* The client you thought loved you and your work actually hates you and your work, or actually loves the paralegal or associate who is staying with your former firm.
* Your client contact does not have authority to take the work from your former firm.
* Your client contact is limited to an approved list of firms.
* Your client's choices include not only you and your former firm, but also other firms and moving work in-house.
* Your client requires technology or other infrastructure that you can no longer provide.
* You misread or misinterpreted what you hoped were positive signals from your client.
* Your former firm makes your client a better deal than you can.
* You walk into a conflict of interest that you did not see coming
* Unbeknownst to you, your former firm blackens your reputation in conversations with the client.

Since you do not have control over these factors, you should—at a minimum—anticipate that they may limit your ability to take clients with you. So be conservative in predicting future business when you start your firm. At the same time, being realistic in the short run doesn't mean that you should write off the prospect of luring in a former firm client entirely. The business of law is competitive and fluid, with companies constantly reevaluating and switching "dance partners." Down the road, a client may expand its list of "approved counsel" to include your new firm. Maybe the great deal that your firm extended to the client will end six months after your departure and the firm decides to look elsewhere. Maybe the CEO of Corporation X retires and the new CEO appoints your once-junior contact as general counsel. One of these days, that ex-client just might give you a call after all.

What's Yours, What's Theirs?

While figuring out the division of clients, departing lawyers must also determine what property they can rightfully take, and what belongs to the firm.

In some instances, technological advancements have mooted the work product question. Most federal courts, and many state courts and administrative agencies, have transitioned to electronic filing. Consequently, you don't need to concern yourself with the ethics of copying your firm's briefs and motions when you can readily access many of them online at the court's Web sites after you leave. But while questions about briefs and memos are easier to resolve, intellectual property issues complicate the question of who owns work product, according to Dennis Kennedy, a legal technology expert and Biglaw lawyer-turned-solo:

> "... In the good old days, a lawyer leaving a firm took work product, forms and other materials. No one gave much thought to this common practice. Today, lawyers create articles, presentations, videos, forms, software applications, Web pages, databases, knowledge-management tools, and other pieces of intellectual property. Firms also realize the value of firm forms, brief banks, handbooks, and the like."

Though intellectual property considerations do not necessarily bar you from taking presentations, forms and software applications that you created for your firm for your own fair use, they may preclude you from licensing or otherwise profiting from those materials. Kennedy notes that many firms have added intellectual property clauses to partnership agreements and advises that, "if you have specific uses planned for materials, be sure to address and document the intellectual property issues."

Equipment and materials. Chances are, your firm equipped you with a laptop, and/or a smartphone, and other technology; the better to keep you tethered to the firm 24/7. Now that you're cutting the ties, expect the firm to cut your service and seek return of its property... though as a partner and part-owner of the firm, you may theoretically have some claim to keeping some of your road warrior gear. As discussed earlier, be sure to copy all vital information from your smartphone and your laptop before giving notice of your departure. As for law books, journals or directories, keep those that came your way by virtue of a bar membership or attendance at a conference. The firm will probably toss those materials anyway.

Special considerations for government lawyers. Lawyers leaving government service to solo don't face the same ethics dilemmas related to client solicitation that confronts their colleagues in private practice. At the same time, government lawyers must deal with ethical restrictions on the "revolving door" between successive government and private employment:

> **ABA Model Rule 1.1** *provides that government lawyers: shall not otherwise represent a client in connection with a matter in which the lawyer participated personally and substantially as a public officer or employee, unless the appropriate government agency gives its informed consent, confirmed in writing, to the representation.*

Most state bars apply a similar "personal and substantial" participation standard, though you should consult applicable rules and bar counsel for further guidance. In addition, lawyers leaving positions with the federal government must comply with the requirements of federal conflict of interest statutes. In addition, some agencies may have their own regulations in addition to restricting lawyers from actively courting clients with cases pending before the agency, or also prohibit lawyers from making personal appearances before the agency for a certain period of time after leaving for the private sector.

While it seems onerous, the "revolving door" regulations may restrict you from handling only a small number of cases.

If you worked as a junior lawyer at a federal agency, you most likely dealt with small, finite matters that concluded before your departure so the players involved would not have a need to hire private counsel. The same is true if you are leaving a prosecutor's office: most of the defendants you prosecuted were probably incarcerated and won't need lawyers, while those in the middle of a case already have representation and, if not, would probably not want to hire the same person who indicted them. And even if you are subject to a bar on personal appearances before an agency for a set time, that still does not preclude you from advising clients on the agency's policies during that time-frame. Even though you are leaving government to start your own firm, consider how large firms deal with conflicts when they hire top agency personnel, a frequently occurring phenomenon.

Government lawyers leave office for private firms all the time, but at a firm other attorneys can handle matters that come before the lawyer's former agency, even if the government lawyer is personally precluded from doing so. At the same time, the former government lawyer adds value, because he can educate other firm lawyers on the agency's regulations and identify appropriate contacts in the agency for further assistance.

In contrast to large firm practice, as a solo, you won't be able to pass off cases that you're disqualified from handling to other lawyers in your firm. But what you can do is establish affiliated networks with other lawyers, or even enter into an "of counsel" relationship. You can then refer clients to these lawyers in your network and provide general consulting and advice while you wait out any cooling period on appearances before the agency. Plus, you can use these affiliations to learn more about fields outside the expertise you gained at government, which will enable you to diversify your practice.

Steps to Take if You Leave the Profession

If you do not plan to practice law anymore, you need to take certain steps to protect yourself and your clients.

Closing an active practice. Ethically, you must be certain that every client you represent with an active case file knows that you are leaving practice, and that they have opportunity to find replacement counsel. You can let them know your recommendation for substitute counsel, but you must obtain their express permission before transferring their case to another lawyer. When you do transfer a file, send it to the new attorney with a cover letter copied to the client. For pending court cases, file a "Notice of Withdrawal and Substitution of Attorney" and make certain opposing counsel receives a copy.

Those clients who want to postpone hiring another lawyer or who can't decide on a replacement can take their files. But before they leave, have them sign a receipt for the file which acknowledges your withdrawal from the case and advice that they promptly find other representation. Then file the "Notice of Withdrawal" with the court and opposing counsel.

Sometimes a court won't allow you to withdraw from an active court case if it would prejudice the client (usually if a hearing or trial is impending). If a court won't permit you to withdraw, you can (1) postpone your departure until every case is concluded; (2) close your office, but make arrangements with another firm to accept pleadings and provide occasional conference room space, or set up a temporary home office or virtual office until you complete the matter; or (3) associate with another lawyer (with your client's permission) and assume the cost of getting the lawyer familiar with the case.

Some states have adopted a version of ABA Model Rule 1.17, allowing a lawyer to sell his or her practice. Research the law in your state before pursuing this course.

Malpractice insurance coverage. Most current policies are "claims made." In other words, you are covered in every annual policy period only for those claims that are actually filed (or sometimes, for those you notified the insurance company might arise in the future). If you have been self-employed or part of a partnership, purchase a "tail" policy (known as an "extended reporting form endorsement"). This policy will protect you against all errors and omissions that occurred before you quit practicing but weren't filed until after you closed your doors. Depending on what you buy, the coverage may last until your death, or for only a limited period. "Tail" policies can cost up to three times the last annual premium, but the investment is essential for peace of mind. On the other hand, if you were a law firm or agency employee, your actions will probably be covered by the continuing policy of your employer— unless they have also dissolved. In that case, make certain that they have purchased the appropriate "tail" coverage. Remember, that if you continue to do a "little bit" of law practicing on the side, you will be personally liable for any claims that arise after policy termination.

Bar association membership. Many former attorneys continue to maintain an active license in at least one jurisdiction. Some remain active in one state and convert to inactive membership elsewhere. Others choose to switch to an inactive membership. If you do choose inactive status, make certain that you know what is required to become active again should you ever need or want to use your license.

By Carolyn Elefant, Esq.
Excerpted from *Solo by Choice 2011/2012: How to Be the Lawyer You Always Wanted to Be*

CHAPTER 18

Your Support Network

Common sense and research both tell us that having a support system is a major benefit in going through a job or any other transition. If you don't have one, either find one or create one. Don't try to do this alone. It helps to have multiple individuals serving different needs, to keep your spirits up and keep you going through the transition period. Because changing jobs or careers is not an easy thing to do. You might make five transitions before you get what you want, and the beginning is slow. You need people to brainstorm with and talk through ideas, to reflect back to you what they see, to encourage you when you get discouraged, and to remind you to take the long-term view.

It's not always easy to find, but try to include in your support group someone who has been through a career transition, knows what it's like, and can offer ideas and support. Most states have lawyer assistance programs that either organize support groups for lawyers in transition, or can serve as a resource to put you in touch with others who are going through or have been through a career transition. Avail yourself of every possible support.

Make sure your support system includes people outside your family. It is possible that your family members may resist your desire for a career change. Change for you likely means change for them—including financial and life-style adjustments that might seem to offer them nothing in return. Be patient with your family and realize that you might have to educate them on why this move would mean a happier you and thus a happier family. However, also realize that if they will be directly affected by your transition, they may not be the most enthusiastic cheerleaders for you at the outset. This is why you need to find people who can be more objective and neutral about the move, while providing you with positive feedback and support.

Some people take advice about support systems lightly and think that they're going to handle it on their own. Lawyers in particular tend to be highly individualistic. But there is nothing about having social support that takes away from your individual achievements. In fact, the opposite might be said to be true. Not only are social connections helpful in keeping your confidence up and keeping you on track toward your goals, they are also an important part of overall life satisfaction. People thrive with strong support systems. And when you have reached your goal of changing jobs and realizing career satisfaction, you will be able to share your success with those who supported you along the way—making your destination all the more satisfying.

"What you can do, or dream you can, begin it.
Boldness has genius, power, and magic in it." —GOETHE

APPENDICES

A 800+ Ways to Use Your Law Degree   *164*

B Legal & Law-Related Certificate & Credential-Building Programs   *174*

C Getting the Most from Career & Outplacement Counseling   *195*

D Homework Assignments   *202*

E The Values Card Sort Exercise   *206*

800+ Ways to Use Your Law Degree

By Richard L. Hermann, Esq.

The following 800+ law-related job titles, arranged into 30 broad career fields, derive from career transitions made by (1) the author's clients, and (2) other attorneys who moved from law to a law-related career and shared their experiences with the author.

Alternative Dispute Resolution

Adjudications Officer (Immigration)
Administrative Judge
Administrative Law Judge
ADR Intake Specialist
Alternative Dispute Resolution Coordinator
Arbitration Administrator
Arbitrator
Asylum Officer
Civil Mediation Program Manager
Community Relations Representative
Conciliator
Consumer Complaints Manager
Contractor Industrial Relations Specialist
Convenor
Court ADR Resources Director
Director of Student Mediation and Dispute
    Resolution
Dispute Resolution Consultant
Dispute Resolution Professional
Domestic Relations Mediation Program
    Manager
Domestic Relations Mediator
Domestic Resolution Specialist
Early Dispute Resolution Manager
Equal Employment Manager (Complaints and
    Resolution)
Fair Housing Specialist
Facilitator
Family Mediator

Family Support Magistrate
Foreclosure Mediator
Health Care Ombudsman
Hearing Officer
Loan Modification Mediator
Mediation Analyst
Mediation Coordinator
Mediation Trainer
Mediator
Neutral Advisor
Ombudsman
Ombudsman for Private Property Rights
Settlement Judge
Small Claims Mediation Program Manager
Small Claims Mediator
Structured Settlements Professional

Civil Rights

Accessibility/Compliance Specialist
Advocacy Coordinator
Affirmative Action Specialist
ADA Coordinator
ADA Compliance Manager
Civil Rights Analyst
Civil Rights Coordinator
Civil Rights/Affirmative Action Investigator
Community Relations Specialist
Conciliation Specialist
Cultural Diversity Director
Equal Opportunity Compliance Specialist

EEO Manager/Officer
Human Rights Administrator
Judiciary AA/EEO Investigator
Legal Compliance Officer

College and University Administration

Law School
Academic Compliance Affairs
Academic Support Program Coordinator
Advocacy Programs Director/Assistant
Career Placement Officer
Career Services Counselor/Officer
Cooperative Legal Education Coordinator
Clinical Program Supervisor
Development/Fundraising
Director of Admissions
Director of Alumni Affairs
Director of Institutional Advancement
Director of Marketing
Director of Student Affairs
Faculty Computer Consultant
Law Librarian
Law Librarian—Electronic Services
Law Information Technology Director
Legal Education Director
Publication Support Specialist
Researcher

Campus Administration
Affirmative Action/EEO Officer
Agricultural Mediation Service Negotiator
Assistant to the President/Chancellor
Athletic Conference Compliance
Business Affairs Director/Officer
Chief of Staff to President
Clinical Risk Specialist
Contract Staff Analyst
Contract Specialist
Compliance Officer
Corporate Liaison Officer
Director of Corporate Compliance
Director of State Compliance
Director of Student Mediation and Dispute
    Resolution
Disability Services Coordinator

Discrimination Investigator
Diversity Management Director
Employee Relations Specialist
Environmental Programs Professional
Equity Coordinator
Estate Recovery Case Coordinator
Ethics Officer
Federal/State Relations Professional
Governance Officer
Grants and Contract Compliance Specialist
Grants and Contracts Manager
Healthcare Licensing Manager
Human Resources Director
Immigration Specialist
Immigration Compliance Officer
International Student Affairs Coordinator
Judicial Affairs Officer
Labor Relations Specialist
Laboratory Business Manager
Land Use Director
Legislative Affairs Professional
Mediator
Ombudsman
Paralegal Program/School Administrator
Planned/Deferred Giving Officer/Director
Policy Development Specialist
Pre-Law Advisor
Public Policy Associate
Real Estate Acquisitions and Leasing Specialist
Real Estate Director/Officer
Real Estate Ventures Director
Risk Manager
Security Compliance Officer
Sexual Harassment Counselor
Sponsored Research Officer
Student Affairs Professional
Student Conflict Resolution Coordinator
Student Legal Affairs Officer
Subcontracts Manager
Technology Licensing Associate
Trademark Licensing Officer
Trust Officer
Trusts and Estates Officer
University Press Legal Editor

College and University Teaching

Law School
Academic Support Instructor
Assistant/Associate/Full Professor
Clinical Program Director
Clinical Program Director/Instructor
Foreign Law School Professor/Lecturer
Legal Research and Writing Instructor

Undergraduate/Graduate
Business Law Professor
Criminal Justice Program Instructor
Dispute Resolution Teacher
Environmental Policy Teacher
Ethics Instructor
Labor Relations Instructor
Law and Anthropology Professor
Law and Economics Professor
Law and History Professor
Law and Psychology Professor
Law and Society Professor
Legal Administration Professor
Legal Studies Program Coordinator
Legal Studies Program Teacher
Paralegal Program Instructor
Real Estate Instructor
Security Assistance Management Instructor
Tax Instructor

Contracts, Procurement, and Grants
Competition Advocate
Contract Negotiator
Contract Administrator/Manager
Contract Specialist/Officer
Contract Staff Analyst
Contract Termination Specialist
Contract and Rights Manager
Federal Contract Compliance EEO Specialist
Grants Administration Specialist
Grants Supervisor
Industrial Property Manager
Master Negotiator
Procurement Officer/Analyst
Purchasing Officer/Director
Self-Determination Specialist

Small Business Advocate
Subcontracts Manager
Technology Transfer Professional
Transactions Coordinator

Corporate, Law Firm and Government Legal Training
Legal Trainer
Persuasion Consultant

Court Administration
ADR Project Coordinator
ADR Resources Director
Alternative Sanctions Coordinator
Assistant Circuit Executive for Legal Affairs
Assistant District Executive for Legal Affairs
Attorney Admissions Deputy
Bankruptcy Administrator
Bankruptcy Appeals Clerk
Bankruptcy Case Administration Manager
Bankruptcy Examiner
Bankruptcy Group Manager
Bar Admissions Administrator
Case Calendaring Clerk
Circuit/District Court Executive
Clerk of Court
Court Administrator
Court Analyst
Court Improvement Programs Manager
Court Mental Health Services Manager
Court Operations Specialist
Court Services Director
Court Technology Advisor
Deputy Clerk
Disciplinary Administrator
Estate/Probate Administrator
Friend of the Court
Government Relations Specialist
Guardian Ad Litem
Guardianship Clerk
Jury Commissioner
Land Commissioner
Legal Documents Officer/Supervisor
Legal Research Director
Legal Researcher
Parole Officer

Pretrial Services Officer
Probation Director
Probation Officer
Public Guardian
Registrar
Reporter of Decisions
Settlement Director
Supervisor of Public Trust Accounts
Support Payments Officer
Training Professional
Victim Services/Restitution Coordinator
Violations Bureau Manager

Criminal Justice and Law Enforcement

Alcohol, Tobacco and Firearms Inspector
Asset Forfeiture Specialist
Bank Fraud Investigator
Border Patrol Agent
Child Abuse Investigator
Child Support Enforcement Case Analyst
Civil Penalties Officer
Civilian Complaint Review Board Officer
Compliance Support Inspector
Computer Crime and Security Specialist
Computer Fraud Investigator
Consumer Safety Inspector
Crime Analyst
Crime Prevention Coordinator
Criminal Investigator
Criminal Justice Administrator/Analyst
Criminal Research Specialist
Customs Inspector
Deputy Inspector General for Investigations
DEA Special Agent
Domestic Investigator
Drug Investigator
Economic Crimes Investigator
Employment Investigator
Enforcement Analyst
Enforcement Professional
FBI Special Agent
Federal Trade Investigator
Financial Enforcement Specialist
Fines, Penalties and Forfeiture Specialist
Foreign Service Narcotics Control Officer
Forensic Investigator

Fraud/White Collar Crime Investigator
Fugitive Witness Investigations Specialist
Game Law Enforcement Officer
General Investigator/Inspector
Hidden Assets Investigator
Immigration Inspector
Inspector General
Inspector General Complaints Analysis
    Specialist
Intellectual Property Loss Investigator
Internal Affairs Director
Investigations Review Specialist
Law Enforcement Coordination Manager
Law Enforcement Specialist
Missing Persons Investigator
Municipal Code Enforcement Officer
Postal Inspector
Private Investigator
Revenue Officer/Agent
Securities Fraud Examiner
Seized Property Specialist
Software Piracy and Licensing Abuse
    Investigator
Special Agent (Wildlife)
Treasury Enforcement Agent
Victims Compensation Officer
Victim Services Manager
Welfare Investigator
White Collar Prison Counselor

Energy and Natural Resources

Carbon Transactions Manager
Compliance Enforcement Analyst
Compliance Enforcement Analyst-Mitigation/
    Reporting
Compliance Program Auditor
Director of Nuclear Licensing
Energy Advocate
Energy Conservation Program Specialist
Energy Efficiency Program Manager
Energy Regulatory Affairs Professional
Energy Trading Compliance Officer
Landman (Oil and Gas)
Land Agent
Manager of Compliance
Mineral Appeals Analyst

Natural Resources Specialist
Nuclear Regulatory Affairs Director
Oil and Gas Leasing Policy Analyst
Public Utilities Specialist
Rate Analyst
Regulatory Projects Manager
Regulatory Representative
Renewable Energy Program Specialist
Right-of-Way Manager
Transmission Right-of-Way Specialist
Utility Contract Administration Analyst

Environmental Careers
Advisor, Regulatory Management
Carbon Transactions Manager
Coastal Zone Resources Manager
Conservation Field Representative
Director of Environmental Affairs
Director, Legislative Analysis Environmental
    Policy Professional
Environmental/Public Health Advocate
Environmental Claims Examiner
Environmental Compliance Manager
Environmental Consultant
Environmental Ombudsman
Environmental Planning Manager
Environmental Policy Analyst
Environmental Protection Specialist
Environmental Public Participation Specialist
Global Government Affairs Director
Hazardous Waste Management Consultant
Land Protection Specialist
Marine Resource Management Specialist
Remediation Specialist
Resource Policy Analyst
Safety and Occupational Health Specialist
Technological Program Hazards Specialist
Trade Association Environmental Staffer

Ethics/Professional Responsibility
Attorney Ethics Coordinator
Attorney Ethics Investigator
Bar Disciplinary Manager
Client Protection Fund Director/Officer
Code of Ethics Compliance Manager
Corporate Ethics Director/Officer

Ethics Advisor
Ethics Auditor
Ethics Commission Director/Officer
Ethics Program Specialist
Ethics Researcher
Ethics Trainer
Governmental Ethics Manager
Health Professions Investigator
Hospital Ethicist
Judicial Disabilities Commission Investigator
Lawyer Assistance Program Director
License Examining Specialist
Manager of Compliance and Ethics
Professional Licensing Officer
Professional Regulation Compliance Analyst
Situational Awareness and Ethics Officer
Unauthorized Practice of Law Advisor
Unauthorized Practice of Law Investigator

Financial Services
Bank International Trade Specialist
Bank Investment Compliance Officer
Bank Probate Administrator/Officer
Banking Enforcement Advisor
Bankruptcy Analyst
Benefits Professional
Capital Market Consultant
Carbon Transactions Manager
Chapter 13 Trustee
Claims/Settlement/Termination Specialist
Commercial Lending Manager
Community Reinvestment Act Director
Compliance Manager
Compliance Officer (Bank Regulation)
Compliance Officer (Commercial Banking)
Compliance Officer (Commodities)
Compliance Officer (Securities)
Compliance Representative
Compliance Trust Officer
Conflicts of Interest Oversight Officer
Consumer Affairs Examiner
Corporate Finance Executive
Credit Examiner
Employee Benefits Trust Administrator
Equities Compliance Officer
Escrow Agent

Estate/Fiduciary Administrator
Estate and Financial Planner
Financial Enforcement Specialist
Financial Institution Examiner
Financial Planner/Planning Analyst
Financial Services Sales Agent
Futures Trading Investigator
Investment Banking Officer
Legal Advertising/Sales Literature Manager
Legal Fee Auditor/Legal Cost Specialist
Legal Product Manager-Corporate
Legal Product Manager-Private Label Funds
Legal Product Manager-Securities/Brokerage
Loan Administrator/Specialist
Loan Workout Officer
Mergers and Acquisitions Specialist
Mutual Fund Administrator
Pension Benefits Examiner
Pension Law Specialist
Probate Accountant
Public Finance Consultant
Regulatory Control Officer
Securities Compliance Examiner
Securities Firm Executive
Securities Transactions Analyst
Trust Advisor
Trust Benefits Specialist
Trust Business Development Professional
Trust Examiner
Trust Officer/Administrator
Trust Property Manager
Trust Risk Analyst
U.S. Trustee/Assistant U.S. Trustee
Workers' Compensation Auditor

Health Care

Contract Negotiator
Director, Pharmaceutical Sales and Marketing
    Compliance
Health Plan Member Services Coordinator
Healthcare Compliance Officer
Healthcare Fraud Investigator
Healthcare Ombudsman
Hospital Planned Giving Professional
Hospital Contracts/Procurement Officer
Hospital Risk Manager

JCAHO Policy Writer
Legal Services Specialist
Nursing Home Investigator
Patient Rights Advocate
Quarantine Investigator
Sanctions Associate

Human Resources

Employee Benefit Plan Specialist
Employee Disability Programs Manager
Employee Relations Manager/Specialist
Employment and Training Specialist
Government Benefits Director
Human Resources Compliance Officer
Human Resources Director
Lawyer Temporary Agency Manager
Legal Career Counselor
Legal Search Consultant
Manpower Development Specialist
Personnel Management Specialist
Professional Standards Administrator
Reemployment Rights Compliance Specialist
Retirement Systems Administrator
Salary Administration Specialist
Social Security Disability Claimant
    Representative
Veterans Program Specialist
Veterans Reemployment Rights Specialist

Human Services

Aging Services Program Specialist
Child Support Collection Specialist
Children's Advocate
Director of Human Relations
Elder Rights Specialist/Advocate
Geriatric Care Manager/Advocate
Long-Term Care Ombudsman
Mental Healthcare Ombudsman
Women's Rights Advocate/
    Domestic Abuse Specialist

Insurance and Risk Management

Bankruptcy Claims Examiner
Casualty Claims Specialist
Civil Service Retirement Claims Examiner
Claims Legal and Regulatory Compliance

Claims Representative/Manager
Commercial Claims Specialist
Dependent and Estates Claims Examiner
Document Compliance Specialist
Environmental Claims Specialist
Errors and Omissions Claims Manager
General Agent
General Claims Examiner
Health Benefits Program Analyst
Health Care Policy Analyst
Health Insurance Specialist
Health Plan Member Services Coordinator
Insurance Agent (Life, Health, and Disability)
Insurance Agent (Property and Casualty)
Insurance Claims Representative
Insurance Consultant
Insurance Fraud Investigator
Insurance Licensing Administrator
Insurance Licensing Consultant
Insurance Market Conduct Examiner
Insurance Officer
Insurance Policy Analyst
Insurance Services Practice Group Head
Insurance Specialist
Issuing Specialist
Liability Claims Analyst
Litigation Examiner
Litigation Manager
Loss and Damage Claims Examiner
Medical Malpractice Claims Analyst
Pension Investigator
Personal Trust Product Manager
Professional Liability Claims Analyst
Professional Liability Insurance Marketer
Professional Liability Underwriter
Recovery Manager
Risk Analyst
Risk Manager
Social Insurance Administrator
Social Insurance Claims Examiner
Transportation Claims Examiner
Unemployment Insurance Administrator
Veterans Claims Examiner
Workers' Compensation Claims Examiner
Workers' Compensation Program Specialist

Intellectual Property

Applications Examiner
Chief Intellectual Property Officer
Chief Strategy Officer
Conveyance Examiner
Copyright Examiner
Corporate Copyright Specialist
Corporate Director of Licensing
Foreign Filing Specialist
Health Care Licensing Manager
Intellectual Asset Manager
Intellectual Property Commercialization
 Specialist
Intellectual Property Director/Manager
Intellectual Property Resources Director
Intellectual Property Rights Enforcement
Intellectual Property Strategist
Licensing Manager/Specialist
Patent Administrator
Patent Analyst
Patent Examiner
Patentability Review Examiner
Patent/Technology Licensing Officer
Rights Manager
Technology Transfer Outreach Professional
Technology Manager—IP
Technology Transfer Director
Trademark Examiner
Trademark Legal Manager

Intelligence/Security

Aviation Security Specialist/Officer
CIA Clandestine Service Agent
Foreign Assets Control Intelligence Analyst
Foreign Service Diplomatic Security Officer
Industrial Property Clearance Specialist
Industrial Security Specialist/Officer
Information Security Consultant
Information Security Specialist/Officer
Intelligence Officer
Intelligence Research Specialist
Internal Security Specialist/Officer
Munitions Export Control Specialist
Personnel Security Specialist/Officer
Physical Security Specialist/Officer
Premises Security Consultant

Security Administration Specialist/Officer
Security Assistance Analyst
Security Classification Specialist/Officer
Security Inspector

International Affairs, Trade, and Investment
Commercial Loan Specialist
Commercial Operations Specialist
Country Risk Analyst
Customs Entry and Liquidation Specialist
Economic Development Director
Economic Development Project Officer
Export Administrator/Manager
Export Control Specialist
Export Credit Manager
Export Factor
Export Insurance Issuing Specialist
Financial Institution Reform Advisor
Foreign Affairs Specialist
Foreign Service Officer
Foreign Trade Zone Manager
Immigration/Benefits Coordinator
Import Compliance Specialist
Import/Export Manager
International Affairs Specialist
International Agency Liaison Officer
International Human Rights Advisor
International Relations Officer
International Trade Specialist
International Trade Consultant
Library Foreign Law Specialist
Manager of Export/Import Compliance
Manager of Global Trading Documentation
Munitions Export Control Specialist
Passport and Visa Examiner
Political Risk Insurance Officer
Tariff and Regulatory Supervisor
Trade Documentation Officer
U.S. Commercial Service Officer

Labor Relations
Industrial Relations Specialist
HR Manager—Labor Relations
Labor Investigator
Labor Management Relations Examiner
Labor Negotiator/Mediator

Labor Relations Clearinghouse Staff
Labor Relations Consultant
Labor Relations Manager/Specialist/Analyst
Labor Relations Planning and Analysis
   Manager
Labor Relations Specialist
NLRB Field Examiner
Wage and Hour Law Administrator
Wage and Hour Law Compliance Specialist

Legal Administration
Bar Association Professional
CLE Administrator
CLE Training Manager/Specialist
Director of Complex Case Support
Director of Knowledge Management
Law Firm Administrator/Executive Director
Law Firm Management Consultant
Law Firm Marketing Director
Law Firm Trainer
Law Firm Recruiter
Legal Services Program Executive Director
Practice Area Coordinator
Pro Bono Coordinator
Professional Relations Coordinator

Legal Documents/Information/Research
Analyst in Social Legislation
Archivist (Legal)
Economic Research Analyst
Freedom of Information/Privacy Officer
Information Management Specialist
Law Librarian
Law Library Computer Network Manager
Legal Database Manager
Legal Historian
Legal Information Analyst
Legal Instruments Examiner
Legal Researcher
Legal Writer
Public Disclosure Officer
Senior Paralegal
Social Science Research Analyst
Technical Legal Information Specialist

Legislative and Regulatory Affairs

Congressional Affairs Specialist
Congressional Inquiries Program Manager
Congressional Liaison Specialist
Food Program Specialist
Governmental Affairs/Relations Positions
Intergovernmental Affairs Specialist
Legislative Affairs Specialist/Legislative Analyst/Legislative Director
Legislative Assistant
Legislative Coordinator
Legislative Correspondent
Legislative Drafter
Legislative Program Manager
Legislative Representative
Legislative Staff Director
Lobbyist
Manager of Regulatory Affairs
Policy Advocate
Policy Analyst
Legislative Committee Staff Member
Program Integrity Specialist
Regulations/Rulings Specialist
Regulatory Analyst
Regulatory Compliance Director
Regulatory Impact Analyst
Regulatory Program Specialist
Regulatory Implementation Manager
Telecommunications Regulatory Analyst

Litigation Management/Support

Alternative Sentencing Consultant
Case Assessment Consultant
Director of Complex Case Support
Jury Selection Advisor
Law Firm Director of Litigation Services
Litigation Analyst
Litigation Management Professional
Litigation Management Trainer
Litigation Support Consultant/Specialist
Litigation Support Project Manager
Trial Consultant

Management and Administration

Acquisitions/Divestiture Professional
Association Executive

Automobile Dealer Performance Manager
City/County Clerk/Administrator
Corporate Secretary
Elections Administration Officer
Emergency Management Specialist
Federal Aid Administrator
Foundation Executive/Program Manager
Grants Management Specialist
Industry Specialist
Law Office Management Specialist
Management Analyst
Nonprofit Advocacy Organization Manager
Program Analyst/Officer
Sports Franchise General Manager
Unclaimed Property Administration

Marketing and Development

Bar Review Regional Director
Business Broker
Gift and Estate Planning Professional
Economic Development Officer
Franchise Development Manager
Law Firm Director of Client Relations
Law Firm Business Development Editor
Law Firm Client Development Director
Legal Cost Management Sales Consultant
Legal Publishing Sales Representative
Public Participation Specialist

Media and Entertainment

Acquisitions Editor
Law Correspondent/Reporter
Law Firm Business Development Editor
Legal Editor
Legal Newspaper/Journal Publisher
Legal Publisher Account Representative
Literary Agent
New Product Development Professional
Public Affairs Specialist
Sports/Talent Agent
Technical Publications Writer/Editor (Legal)

Real Estate/Housing

Community Development Block Grant Coordinator
Development Specialist

Director of Real Estate
Fair Housing Community Educator
Fair Housing Test Coordinator
Housing Advocate
Housing Authority Director/Professional
Housing Programs Administrator
Housing Services Planner
Land Agent
Land Acquisition Manager
Land Law Examiner
Land Manager
Land Preservation Director
Land Protection Director/Specialist
Lease Negotiator
Real Estate Auction Project Manager
Realty Specialist/Officer
Register of Deeds
Right-of-Way Agent
Tenant's Broker
Title Examiner
Zoning Administrator

Taxation

Estate Tax Examiner
International Tax Analyst
Property and Transaction Tax Manager
Tax Agent
Tax Compliance Manager
Tax Law Specialist
Tax Manager/Tax Planning Manager
Tax Research Manager/Professional
Technical Services Manager
Trust Tax Manager

Transportation

Admeasurer
Boating Law Administrator
Highway Safety Specialist
Marine Inspector
Marine Transportation Policy Analyst
Traffic Management Specialist
Transportation Specialist
Transportation Safety Consultant
Trucking Compliance Specialist
Vessel Traffic Specialist

By Richard L. Hermann, Esq.
Excerpt, *From Lemons to Lemonade in the New Legal Job Market* (2012)

Legal & Law-Related Certificate & Credential-Building Programs

By Richard L. Hermann, Esq.

Two things are important to note when considering the following list: credentialing programs are in constant flux. It is likely that there will be changes to certain programs and their web addresses between the time this list was prepared and publication of this book. Secondly, certain programs require that you meet minimum threshold qualification requirements in order to enroll. These are always explained on the program's Web site:

Alternative Dispute Resolution

- American Arbitration Association Programs (www.adr.org)
- Association for Conflict Resolution (www.acrnet.org). Approved Family Mediation Training Programs
- Boise State University—Certificate in Dispute Resolution (www.boisestate.edu)
- Center for Legal Studies (www.legalstudies.com). Alternative Dispute Resolution Certificate (online option)
- Hamline University School of Law (www.hamline.edu/law). (1) Certificate in Dispute Resolution; (2) Certificate in Global Arbitration Law and Practice
- Hawaii Pacific University (www.hpu.edu). (1) Certificate in Mediation and Conflict (online); (2) Commercial Mediation Certification (online); (3) Commercial Arbitration Certification (online)
- Institute for Conflict Resolution (www.icmadr.com). Family Mediation Certification (online)
- Marquette University (www.marquette.edu). Graduate Certificate in Dispute Resolution
- Marylhurst University (www.marylhurst.edu). Certificate in Conflict Resolution & Mediation (online)
- Mediation Matters (www.mediationmatters.com/training.html). (1) Basic Mediation Training; (2) Business and Employment Mediation Training; (3) Divorce Mediation Training; (4) Marital Property Mediation Training; (5) Child Access Mediation Training

- Mountain States Employers' Council (www.msec.org). Mediating Workplace Disputes
- New York University (www.nyu.edu). Certificate in Conflict & Dispute Resolution
- Northeastern University (www.cps.neu.edu/programs/certificates/). Conflict Resolution Studies Certificate
- Northern Virginia Mediation Service (www.nvms.us). Virginia Mediator Certification
- Southern Methodist University (www.smu.edu). Dispute Resolution Graduate Certificate Program
- World Trade Organization (www.wto.org). (1) Dispute Settlement System Training Module; (2) General Agreement on Trade in Services

Art & Museums
- Boston University (www.bu.edu). Metropolitan College—Graduate Certificate in Arts Administration
- DePaul University College of Law (www.law.depaul.edu). Certificate in Intellectual Property: Arts & Museum Law
- Harvard College (www.harvard.edu). Certificate in Museum Studies

Banking & Finance
- American Institute of Banking (www.aba.com). (1) AIB Banking and Finance Diploma; (2) AIB Personal Trust Diploma
- Association of Certified Anti-Money Laundering Specialists (http://www.acams.org/). Certified Anti-Money Laundering Specialist (online)
- Boston University (www.bu.edu). Metropolitan College—Graduate Diploma Program in Banking and Financial Services
- Credit Union National Association (http://training.cuna.org). Regulatory Training & Certification Program
- Florida International University (http://business.fiu.edu). Certificate in Banking
- Hedge Funds Association (www.hedge-funds-association.com). Certified Hedge Fund Compliance Expert (CHFCE)(online)
- Institute of Certified Bankers (www.aba.com/ICBCertifications). (1) Certified Regulatory Compliance Manager (CRCM); (2) Certified Corporate Trust Specialist (CCTS)
- Keller Graduate School of Management of DeVry University (www.directdegree.com). Graduate Certificate in Financial Analysis
- Lorman Education Services (www.lorman.com). Certificate of Banking Compliance
- Northeastern University (www.cps.neu.edu/programs/certificates/). Financial Institutions and Markets Certificate
- University of the Pacific (www.pacific.edu). Banking Leadership Certificate Program

Bankruptcy Law
- American Board of Certification (www.abcworld.org). (1) Business Bankruptcy Certificate; (2) Consumer Bankruptcy Certificate; (3) Creditors' Rights Law Certificate

Bioethics

- Indiana University (www.iupui.edu). Purdue University Indianapolis—Bioethics Certificate
- Loyola University Chicago (http://bioethics.lumc.edu/online_masters.html). Certificate in Bioethics and Health Policy (online)
- Medical College of Wisconsin (www.mcw.edu). Certificate in Clinical Bioethics Program (online)
- Montefiore Medical Center (www.montefiore.org). Montefiore-Einstein Certificate Program in Bioethics and Medical Humanities
- Union Graduate College (www.bioethics.union.edu). Mount Sinai School of Medicine—Certificate in Bioethics: (1) Specialization in Clinical Ethics; (2) Specialization in Research Ethics; (3) Specialization in Health Policy & Law
- University of Nevada, Reno (www.unr.edu). Graduate Certificate in Bioethics, Bioterrorism Preparedness
- Penn State University (www.worldcampus.psu.edu/certificates.shtml). Certificate in Bioterrorism Preparedness (online)
- Georgetown University (http://grad.georgetown.edu/pages/certif_biohazard.cfm). (1) Biohazardous Threat Agents and Emerging Infectious Diseases Certificate Program (online); (2) Biodefense and Public Policy Certificate

Child Welfare Law

- National Association of Counsel for Children (www.naccchildlaw.org). Certified Child Welfare Law Specialist
- Center for Guardianship Certification (www.guardianshipcert.org). (1) Registered Guardian Certification; (2) Master Guardian Certification

Climate Change

- University of California (http://unex.uci.edu). Irvine Extension—Decision Making for Climate Change (online) [in conjunction with the University of Washington Educational Outreach, Northwestern University School of Continuing Studies and the University of British Columbia Continuing Studies]

Compliance

- ABS Consulting (www.absconsulting.com). (1) Environmental and Quality Certification Programs; (2) Clean Air Compliance (CAC) Specialist; (3) Clean Water Compliance (CWC) Specialist: (4) EMS Compliance (EMSC) Specialist; (5) Hazardous Waste Compliance (HWC) Specialist; (6) QMS Compliance (QMSC) Specialist; (7) Regulatory Compliance Specialist (RCS)
- Association of Health Care Compliance Professionals (www.hcca-info.org). Certificate in Healthcare Compliance
- Compliance LLC (www.compliance-llc.com). (1) Certified Basel ii Professional (online); (2) Certified Sarbanes Oxley Expert (online); (3) Certified Risk and Compliance Management Professional (online)
- Compliance Resources (www.complianceresources.com). (1) Certified Healthcare Compliance Officer (CHCO)(online); (2) Certified Healthcare Compliance Consultant (CHCC)(online)

- Credit Union National Association (http://training.cuna.org). Regulatory Training & Certification Program
- Financial Industry Regulatory Authority (www.finra.com). FINRA Compliance Boot Camp
- Florida Gulf Coast University (www.fgcu.edu). Graduate Compliance Certificate Program (online)
- George Washington University (www.gwu.edu). Graduate Certificate in Healthcare Corporate Compliance
- Hamline University School of Law (http://law.hamline.edu). Health Care Compliance Certification Program
- Health Care Compliance Association (http://hcca-info.org). (1) Certified in Healthcare Compliance Professional (CHC); (2) Healthcare Research Compliance Certification (CHRC); (3) Certified in Healthcare Compliance Fellowship (CHC-F)
- Hedge Funds Association (www.hedge-funds-association.com). Certified Hedge Fund Compliance Expert (CHFCE)(online)
- Institute of Certified Bankers (www.aba.com/ICBCertifications). Certified Regulatory Compliance Manager (CRCM)
- International Import-Export Institute (http://expandglobal.com). Certified U.S. Export Compliance Officer
- LOMA (www.loma.org). Associate, Insurance Regulatory Compliance® (AIRC) (online)
- Lorman Education Services (www.lorman.com). (1) Certificate of Banking Compliance; (2) Construction Compliance Certification
- National Regulatory Services (www.nrs-inc.com). Investment Adviser Compliance Certificate Program
- National Safety Council (www.nsc.org). Certificate in OSHA Compliance
- Purdue University (www.purdue.edu). Regulatory & Quality Compliance Graduate Certificate Program
- St. Thomas University (FL) School of Law (www.stu.edu/lawschool). International Tax Law Program: Anti-Money Laundering & Compliance Certificate
- Seton Hall University School of Law (www.law.shu.edu). Health Care Compliance Certification Program
- Sheshunoff (www.sheshunoff.com). Regulatory Compliance Certification Program
- Society of Corporate Compliance & Ethics (www.corporatecompliance.org). (1) Certified Compliance & Ethics Professional; (2) Certified Compliance and Ethics Professional-Fellow
- Quinnipiac University (www.quinnipiac.edu). Healthcare Compliance Certificate
- University of Washington Extension (www.extension.washington.edu). Certificate Program in Healthcare Regulatory Compliance

Construction Law
- Lorman Education Services (www.lorman.com). Construction Compliance Certification

- University of California at Davis (http://extension.ucdavis.edu). Certificate Program in Construction Management

Consulting
- Nexient Learning (www.nexientlearning.com). Associate Certificate in Consulting
- Kaplan University (www.kaplan.edu). Legal Nurse Consulting Certificate
- American Association of Legal Nurse Consultants (www.aalnc.org). Legal Nurse Consultant Certificate

Contracts & Procurement
- Villanova University (www.villanova.edu). Master Certificate in Government Contract Management (online)
- University of Virginia (www.uva.edu). Graduate Certificate Program in Procurement and Contracts Management
- National Contract Management Association (www.ncmahq.org). (1) Certified Commercial Contracts Manager; (2) Certified Professional Contracts Manager; (3) Certified Federal Contracts Manager

Corporate Governance
- Compliance LLC (www.compliance-llc.com). Certified Sarbanes Oxley Expert (online)
- University of North Carolina Greensboro (www.uncg.edu). Corporate Governance & Ethics Certificate
- Harvard Business School Executive Education (www.exed.hbs.edu). Corporate Governance Series
- Tulane University (www.corpgovonline.com). Excellence in Corporate Governance Certificate
- New York University School of Continuing and Professional Studies (http://www.scps.nyu.edu). Certificate in Ethics and Corporate Governance

Corporate Restructuring
- Association of Insolvency & Restructuring Advisors (www.airacira.org). Certified Insolvency & Restructuring Advisor (CIRA)
- Association of Certified Turnaround Professionals (www.actp.org). Certified Turnaround Professional
- Post University Online (www.post.edu/online). Graduate Certificate in Corporate Innovation (online)

Counseling
- University of California—Santa Cruz (www.ucsc.edu). Human Services Certificate in Counseling
- Capella University (www.capella.edu). Graduate Certificate in Professional Counseling

Creditors' Rights

- American Board of Certification (www.abcworld.org). Creditors' Rights Law Certificate

Criminal Justice

- National Board of Trial Advocacy (www.nbtanet.org). Criminal Trial Certificate (online)
- Association of Certified Fraud Examiners (www.acfe.com). Certified Fraud Examiner
- University of Massachusetts(http://umass.edu). Criminal Justice Studies Certificate
- Post University Online (www.post.edu/online). Criminal Justice Certificate in Homeland Security (online)
- Boston University—Metropolitan College (www.bu.edu). Criminal Justice Certificate Program
- Utica College (www.utica.edu). Financial Crimes Investigator Certificate (online)
- Northeastern University (www.spcs.neu.edu). Graduate Certificate in Community Justice Studies
- Association of Certified Anti-Money Laundering Specialists (www.acams.org). Anti-Money Laundering Specialist Certificate
- University of Virginia in conjunction with the Federal Bureau of Investigation (www.uva.edu). Certificate Program in Criminal Justice Education
- California State University at Fullerton(www.csufextension.org). Certificate in Crime and Intelligence Analysis

Disability Law

- National Board of Trial Advocacy (www.nbtanet.org). Social Security Disability Certificate (online)
- University of Illinois—Chicago (www.uic.edu). Disability Ethics Certificate Program
- Mountain States Employers' Council (www.msec.org). Americans with Disabilities Act: Managing Disabilities in the Workplace
- National Board of Social Security Disability Advocacy (www.nblsc.us). Social Security Disability Specialist

E-Commerce

- University of Virginia (www.uva.edu). Graduate Certificate Program in E-Commerce
- Eastern Michigan University (www.emich.edu). Graduate Certificate in E-Business
- Keller Graduate School of Management of DeVry University (www.directdegree. com). Graduate Certificate in Electronic Commerce Management (online)

E-Discovery/IT/Records Management

- University of Washington Extension (www.extension.washington.edu/ext/ certificates/edm/edm_gen.asp). Certificate in Electronic Discovery Management

- California State University at Fullerton (www.csufextension.org). Certificate in Electronic Discovery
- AIIM—The Enterprise Content Management Association (www.aiim.org). Electronic Records Management Certificate Program (online)
- Keller Graduate School of Management of DeVry University (www.directdegree.com). (1) Graduate Certificate in Information Security (online); (2) Graduate Certificate in Information Systems Management (online)
- Association of Record Managers & Administrators (www.arma.org). Certified Records Manager
- Stevens Institute of Technology Web Campus (http://webcampus.stevens.edu/Legal-Issues-IT.aspx). Legal Issues in IT Graduate Certificate (online)

Economic Development
- Penn State University (www.worldcampus.psu.edu/certificates.shtml). Certificate in Community and Economic Development (online)
- National Development Council (http://nationaldevelopmentcouncil.org/index.php/site/training_schedule/category/certification/). Economic Development Finance Professional Certification Program™

Education Law
- Student Affairs Administrators in Higher Education (www.naspa.org). NASPA Certificate Program in Student Affairs Law and Policy
- National Alliance for Insurance Education and Research (www.scic.com/CRM/CRMmain.htm). Certified School Risk Manager (CSRM) [California and Texas only]

Elder Law and Affairs
- National Elder Law Foundation (www.nelf.org). Certified Elder Law Attorney
- Marylhurst University (www.marylhurst.edu). Graduate Certificate in Gerontology (online)
- University of Toledo (www.utoledo.edu). Elder Law Graduate Certificate Online (online)

Emergency Management
- American Military University (www.amu.apus.edu). Graduate Certificate in Emergency and Disaster Management
- Penn State University (www.worldcampus.psu.edu/certificates.shtml). Graduate Certificate in Disaster Preparedness (online)
- Emergency Management Institute (http://training.fema.gov/EMI/). 50 Certificate Programs

Employee Benefits
- Georgetown University Law Center (www.law.georgetown.edu). Employee Benefits Law Certificate
- John Marshall Law School (www.jmls.edu). Graduate Certificate in Employee Benefits Law

- Temple University, James E. Beasley School of Law (www.law.temple.edu). Employee Benefits Certificate Program
- Villanova University School of Law (www.law.villanova.edu). Employee Benefits Certificate
- eCornell (www.ecornell.com). Benefits and Compensation Online Certificate
- Mountain States Employers' Council (www.msec.org). Compensation and Benefits Certificate Program
- Department of Veterans Affairs (www.va.gov). Accredited Veterans Benefits Representative
- Institute for Applied Management and Law (www.iaml.com). Certificate in Employee Benefits Law℠ Seminar

Energy & Natural Resources
- University of Vermont Law School (www.vermontlaw.edu). Summer Energy Programs
- University of Denver, Sturm College of Law (www.law.du.edu). Certificate of Studies (CS) in Natural Resources Law and Policy
- University of Houston Bauer College of Business (www.bauer.uh.edu). (1) Energy Risk Management Certificate; (2) Energy Investment Analysis Certificate; (3) Energy Finance Certificate
- University of California-Davis Extension (http://extension.ucdavis.edu/certificates/). (1) Energy Resource Management Certificate (online); (2) Certificate Program in Renewable Energy (partially online)
- American Association of Professional Landmen (www.aapl.org). (1) Certified Professional Landman; (2) Registered Professional Landman Designation (www.nea.fr/html/law/isnl/index.html). (3) Registered Landman Designation
- Centenary College—Graduate Certificate in Oil & Gas Management (www.centenary.edu)
- International School of Nuclear Law—Introductory Course on Nuclear Law

Entertainment, Sports & Media
- UCLA Anderson School of Management (www.anderson.ucla.edu). Summer Intensive Certificate Program in Entertainment/Media Management
- American Military University (www.amu.apus.edu). (1) Graduate Certificate in Athletic Administration; (2) Graduate Certificate in Sports Management
- Southern New Hampshire University (www.snhu.edu). (1) International Sport Management Graduate Certificate (online); (2) Sport Management Graduate Certificate (online)
- United States Sports Academy (www.ussa.edu). Sports Management Certificates: (1) Sports Administration (online); (2) Sports Agents (online); (3) Sports Law and Risk Management (online); (4) Sports Business (online)
- National Football League Players Association (www.nflplayers.com). (1) Agent Certification; (2) Player Financial Advisor Registration
- National Basketball Players Association (www.nbpa.org). NBPA Player Agent Certification

- Columbia Southern University (www.columbiasouthern.edu). Certificate in Sport Management (online)

Environmental Law & Regulation
- Harvard University (www.extension.harvard.edu). Certificate in Environmental Management (online)
- University of Denver University College (www.universitycollege.du.edu). Environmental Policy Certificate
- University of Colorado (www.colorado.edu). Graduate Certificate in Environment, Policy, and Society
- Pace Law School (www.law.pace.edu). Certificate in Environmental Law
- Tufts Institute of the Environment (www.tufts.edu/tie). Certificate in Environmental Management
- University of Georgia (www.uga.edu). Environmental Ethics Certificate Program
- University of Washington Extension (www.extension.washington.edu). Certificate Program in Environmental Law and Regulation
- The Academy of Board Certified Environmental Professionals (www.abcep.org). Certified Environmental Professional Designation
- National Registry of Environmental Professionals (www.nrep.org). (1) Registered Environmental Manager Certificate; (2) Associate Environmental Professional Certificate
- ABS Consulting (www.absconsulting.com). Environmental and Quality Certification Programs: (1) Clean Air Compliance (CAC) Specialist; (2) Clean Water Compliance (CWC) Specialist; (3) EMS Compliance (EMSC) Specialist; (4) Hazardous Waste Compliance (HWC) Specialist; (5) QMS Compliance (QMSC) Specialist; (6) Regulatory Compliance Specialist (RCS)
- Johns Hopkins University Bloomberg School of Public Health (http://commprojects.jhsph.edu/academics/Certificate.cfm). Humane Sciences and Toxicology Policy Certificate
- United Nations Educational, Scientific and Cultural Organization (www.unesco.org). Water & Environmental Law and Institutions
- University of California-Davis Extension (http://extension.ucdavis.edu/certificates/). Certificate in Land Use and Environmental Planning

Estate Planning, Planned Giving & Trusts
- National Association of Estate Planners & Councils (www.naepc.org). (1) Estate Planning Law Specialist; (2) Accredited Estate Planner
- Georgetown University Law Center (www.law.georgetown.edu). Estate Planning Certificate
- St. Thomas University (FL) School of Law (www.stu.edu/lawschool). Certificate in the International Tax Law Program:
- Capital University Law School (www.law.capital.edu). Certificate in Estate Planning
- Temple University, James E. Beasley School of Law (www.law.temple.edu). Estate Planning Certificate Program

- Villanova University School of Law (www.law.villanova.edu). Estate Planning Certificate
- College of William & Mary (www.wm.edu). Certificate in Planned Giving
- American Institute of Banking (www.aba.com). AIB Personal Trust Diploma
- Institute of Certified Bankers (www.aba.com/ICBCertifications). (1) Certified Corporate Trust Specialist (CCTS); (2) Certified Trust and Financial Advisor (CTFA)
- University of Washington—Tacoma—Fundraising Management Certificate (www.tacoma.washington.edu/pdc/schedule/fundraising_cert.html)

Ethics
- University of North Carolina (www.uncg.edu). Greensboro—Corporate Governance & Ethics Certificate
- University of New Mexico (www.unm.edu). (1) Business Ethics Certificate Program; (2) Health Care Ethics Certificate Program
- University of Illinois—Chicago—Disability Ethics Certificate Program (www.uic.edu)
- Southern Methodist University—Accounting Ethics Certificate Program (www.smu.edu)
- University of Florida—Pharmacy Law and Ethics Certificate Program (www.ufl.edu)
- University of Georgia—Environmental Ethics Certificate Program (www.uga.edu)
- Public Responsibility in Medicine and Research (PRIM&R)—(1) Certified Institutional Review Board Professional (CIP®); (2) Certified Professional Institutional Animal Care & Use Committee Administrator (CPIA) (www.primr.org)
- Society of Corporate Compliance & Ethics—Certified Compliance & Ethics Professional (www.corporatecompliance.org)

Family Law
- National Board of Trial Advocacy (www.nbtanet.org). Family Law Certificate (online)
- Association for Conflict Resolution (www.acrnet.org). Approved Family Mediation Training Programs

Food, Drugs & Devices
- University of Maryland (www.umd.edu). Graduate Certificate of Professional Studies in Food Safety Risk Analysis
- Michigan State University (www.msu.edu). International Food Law Internet Certificate Program
- Purdue University (www.purdue.edu). Regulatory & Quality Compliance Graduate Certificate Program
- Temple University Quality Assurance & Regulatory Affairs Graduate Program (www.temple.edu). (1) Drug Development Certificate; (2) Clinical Trial Management; (3) Medical Device Certificate

- University of Florida (www.ufl.edu). Pharmacy Law and Ethics Certificate Program
- Northeastern University (www.spcs.neu.edu). (1) Biopharmaceutical Domestic Regulatory Affairs (online option); (2) Biopharmaceutical International Regulatory Affairs (online option); (3) Medical Devices Regulatory Affairs (online option))

Fraud Investigation
- Association of Certified Fraud Examiners (www.acfe.com). Certified Fraud Examiner
- Utica College (www.utica.edu). Financial Crimes Investigator Certificate (online)
- Association of Certified Anti-Money Laundering Specialists (www.acams.org). Anti-Money Laundering Specialist Certificate
- California State University at Fullerton (www.csufextension.org). Certificate in Healthcare Fraud and Abuse in the Application of Medical Coding (online)

Globalization
- Thunderbird School of Global Management (www.thunderbird.edu). Globalization: Merging Strategy with Action

Grants Management
- Management Concepts (www.managementconcepts.com). Grants Management Certificate Program

Guardianship
- Center for Guardianship Certification (www.guardianshipcert.org). (1) Registered Guardian Certification; (2) Master Guardian Certification

Health Law & Administration
- George Washington University Law School (www.law.gwu.edu). (1) Graduate Certificate in Public Health; (2) Graduate Certificate in Healthcare Corporate Compliance
- DePaul University College of Law (www.law.depaul.edu). Certificate in Health Law
- Seton Hall University School of Law (www.law.shu.edu). Health Care Compliance Certification Program
- University of Maryland (www.umd.edu). Graduate Certificate of Professional Studies in Food Safety Risk Analysis
- University of Florida (www.ufl.edu). Graduate Certificate in Health Care Risk Management
- Kaplan University (www.kaplan.edu). Legal Nurse Consulting Certificate
- University of New Mexico (www.unm.edu). Health Care Ethics Certificate Program
- Mountain States Employers' Council (www.msec.org). HIPAA: Privacy Rules and Portability
- Florida International University Legal Studies Institute (www.fiu.edu). Medical/Legal Consultant Certificate

- American College of Healthcare Executives (www.ache.org). Fellows Program
- American Association of Legal Nurse Consultants (www.aalnc.org). Legal Nurse Consultant Certificate
- The Association of Health Care Compliance Professionals (www.hcca-info.org). Certificate in Healthcare Compliance
- American Hospital Association Certification Center (www.aha.org). Certified Professional in Healthcare Risk Management (online)
- Healthcare Quality Certification Board (www.cphq.org). Certified Professional in Healthcare Quality (online)
- Center for Insurance Education & Professional Development (www.insuranceeducation.org) Long-Term Care Professional (LTCP) Designation
- Cleveland State University (www.csuohio.edu/ce). Patient Advocacy Certificate Program (online)
- National Safety Council (www.nsc.org). Certificate in OSHA Compliance
- University of Washington Extension (www.extension.washington.edu). Certificate Program in Healthcare Regulatory Compliance
- Quinnipiac University (www.quinnipiac.edu). Healthcare Compliance Certificate
- Johns Hopkins University (http://commprojects.jhsph.edu/academics/Certificate.cfm). Certificate in Health Policy
- American Society for Healthcare Risk Management (www.ashrm.org). Barton Certificate Program in Healthcare Risk Management
- Northeastern University (www.spcs.neu.edu). (1) Biopharmaceutical Domestic Regulatory Affairs (online option); (2) Biopharmaceutical International Regulatory Affairs (online option); (3) Medical Devices Regulatory Affairs (online option)
- University of California-Davis Extension (http://extension.ucdavis.edu/certificates/). (1) Health Informatics Certificate Program (online); (2) Intensive Certificate Program in Workplace Health and Safety
- California State University at Fullerton (www.csufextension.org). Certificate in Healthcare Fraud and Abuse in the Application of Medical Coding (online)
- Compliance Resources (www.complianceresources.com). (1) Certified Healthcare Compliance Officer (CHCO)(online); (2) Certified Healthcare Compliance Consultant (CHCC)(online)
- Health Care Compliance Association (http://hcca-info.org). (1) Certified in Healthcare Compliance Professional (CHC); (2) Healthcare Research Compliance Certification (CHRC); (3) Certified in Healthcare Compliance Fellowship (CHC-F)
- Hamline University School of Law (http://law.hamline.edu). Health Care Compliance Certification Program
- City University of New York (www.workered.org). The Murphy Institute—The Graduate Certificate in Health Care Policy and Administration

Historic Preservation
- University of Hawaii (www.hawaii.edu). Graduate Certificate in Historic Preservation
- University of North Carolina-Greensboro (www.uncg.org). Post-Baccalaureate Certificate in Historic Preservation

Human Resources

- Society for Human Resource Management (www.shrm.org). (1) Professional in Human Resources; (2) Senior Professional in Human Resources
- Southern New Hampshire University (www.snhu.edu). Certificate in Human Resources Management (online)
- Human Capital Institute (www.hci.org). Human Capital Strategist Designation
- Villanova University (www.villanova.edu). Master Certificate in Human Resource Management (online)
- Cornell University (www.cornell.edu). (1) Human Resources Management Certificate (online); (2) HR: Benefits and Compensation Certificate (online)
- Strayer University (http://strayer.edu-info.com). Executive Graduate Certificate in Business Administration—Human Resource Management

Human Rights

- Center for International Humanitarian Cooperation (www.cihc.org). (1) International Diploma in Humanitarian Assistance; (2) Humanitarian Negotiators Training Course; (3) Forced Migration Program
- Columbia University Continuing Education (http://ce.columbia.edu). Human Rights Certificate Program
- University of Iowa Center for Human Rights (http://international.uiowa.edu). Certificate in Human Rights
- University of Cincinnati (www.uc.edu). International Human Rights Certificate

Insurance & Risk Management

- Kaplan University (www.kaplan.edu). Risk Management Certificate (online)
- American Institute for CPCU & Insurance Institute of America (www.aicpcu.org). (1) Associate in Risk Management (ARM); (2) Associate in Risk Management for Public Entities (ARM-P)
- Compliance LLC (www.compliance-llc.com).Certified Risk and Compliance Management Professional (online)
- National Alliance for Insurance Education and Research (www.scic.com/CRM/CRMmain.htm). (1) Certified Risk Manager (CRM); (2) Certified School Risk Manager (CSRM)[California and Texas only]
- Stanford University (www.stanford.edu). Certificate Program: Strategic Decision and Risk Management
- Institute of Risk Management (www.theirm.org). Certificate in Risk Management
- University of Maryland (www.umd.edu). Graduate Certificate of Professional Studies in Food Safety Risk Analysis
- University of Florida (www.ufl.edu). Graduate Certificate in Health Care Risk Management
- Mountain States Employers' Council (www.msec.org). Workplace Risk Management Certificate Program
- University of Houston Bauer College of Business (www.bauer.uh.edu). Energy Risk Management Certificate
- American Hospital Association Certification Center (www.aha.org). Certified Professional in Healthcare Risk Management (online)

- American Society for Healthcare Risk Management (www.ashrm.org). Barton Certificate Program in Healthcare Risk Management
- Professional Risk Managers International Association (www.prima.org). Professional Risk Manager (PRM™) Certification Program
- LOMA (www.loma.org). Associate, Insurance Regulatory Compliance® (online)
- Boston University Distance Education (http://www.bu.edu/online/online_programs/certificate_programs/). Online Graduate Certificate in Risk Management and Organizational Continuity (online)
- Institute of Consumer Financial Information (www.icfe.us). Certified Identity Theft Risk Management Specialist

Intellectual Property
- DePaul University College of Law (www.law.depaul.edu). (1) Certificate in Intellectual Property: Arts & Museum Law; (2) Certificate in Intellectual Property: General; (3) Certificate in Intellectual Property: Patents
- Licensing Executives Society (www.usa-canada.les.org). Intellectual Asset Management Certificates
- Franklin Pierce Law Center (www.piercelaw.edu). Intellectual Property Diploma
- U.S. Department of Agriculture Graduate School (www.grad.usda.gov). Technology Transfer Program
- University of California, Berkeley Extension (www.unex.berkeley.edu). Certificate in Technology Transfer and Commercialization
- World Intellectual Property Organization (www.wipo.int). (1) Primer on Intellectual Property (online); (2) General Course on Intellectual Property (online); (3) Introduction to the Patent Cooperation Treaty (online); (4) Copyright and Related Rights (online); (5) Biotechnology and Intellectual Property (online); (6) Patents (online); (7) Trademarks, Industrial Designs and Geographic Indications (online); (8) Arbitration and Mediation Procedure Under the WIPO Rules (online); (9) Patent Information Search (online); (10) Basics of Patent Drafting (online)
- University of San Diego (www.sandiego.edu). Intellectual Property Professional Certificate
- Northeastern University (www.spcs.neu.edu). Graduate Certificate in Intellectual Property
- New York University School of Continuing and Professional Studies (http://www.scps.nyu.edu). Certificate in Intellectual Property Law
- Foundation for Advanced Education in the Sciences (http://faes.org/grad/certificate_programs/technology_transfer). Technology Transfer Certificate Program

Intelligence, Homeland Security & National Security
- Texas A&M University (www.tamu.edu). (1) Graduate Certificate in Homeland Security; (2) Certified Training Professional
- Post University Online (www.post.edu/online). Criminal Justice Certificate in Homeland Security

- Michigan State University (www.msu.edu). Online Certificate in Homeland Security Studies
- Point Park University (www.pointpark.edu). Certificate in Intelligence and National Security
- University of New Haven (www.newhaven.edu). National Security Certificate
- American Military University (www.amu.apus.edu). (1) Graduate Certificate in Homeland Security; (2) Graduate Certificate in Intelligence Studies; (3) Graduate Certificate in National Security Studies
- George Washington University (www.gwu.edu). International Security Policy Certificate
- Long Island University (www.southampton.liu.edu). Advanced Certificate in Homeland Security Management (online)
- Penn State University (www.worldcampus.psu.edu/certificates.shtml). (1) Certificate in Bioterrorism Preparedness (online); (2) Graduate Certificate in Disaster Preparedness (online)
- Eastern Kentucky University (www.eku.edu). Certificate in Homeland Security (online)

International Affairs & Business
- St. Thomas University (FL) School of Law (www.stu.edu/lawschool). Certificates in the International Tax Law Program: (1) International Financial Centers; (2) United States Taxation; (3) E-Commerce; (4) Anti-Money Laundering & Compliance; (5) Trusts and Estate Planning
- Illinois Institute of Technology, Chicago-Kent College of Law (www.kentlaw.edu). Certificate in International Law & Practice
- Hamline University School of Law (www.hamline.edu/law). Certificate in Global Arbitration Law and Practice
- Pace Law School (www.law.pace.edu). Certificate in International Law
- Ellis College of New York Institute of Technology (http://ellis.nyit.edu). Graduate Certificate-International Business (online)
- University of Maryland University College (www.umuc.edu). Certificate in International Trade (online)
- World Trade Organization (www.wto.org). (1) Dispute Settlement System Training Module; (2) General Agreement on Trade in Services
- University of the Pacific (http://web.pacific.edu). International Trade Certificate Program
- Berkeley City College (http://berkeley.peralta.edu). International Trade Certificate of Completion
- Long Island University (www.liu.edu). United Nations Advanced Certificate (on-line)
- International Import-Export Institute (http://expandglobal.com). (1) Certified International Trade Law Specialist; (2) Certified U.S. Export Compliance Officer; (3) Certified International Trade Manager; (4) Certified International Trade Professional; (5) Certified International Trade Marketing Specialist; (6) Certified International Trade Documentation Specialist; (7) Certified International Trade

Logistics Specialist; (8) Certified International Trade Finance Specialist;
(9) Certified Exporter; (10) Certified International Trade Educator
- International Maritime Law Institute (www.imli.org). (1) Certificate: General
Introduction to Public International Law; (2) Certificate: The Law of International
Institutions; (3) Certificate: Introduction to Shipping Law; (4) Certificate:
International Marine Environmental Law; (5) Certificate: Maritime Legislation
Drafting; (6) Certificate: EC Maritime and Shipping Law; (7) International Law of
the Sea Certificates: (a) Introduction to the International Law of the Sea;
(b) The High Seas Legal Status and Freedoms; (c) Common Heritage of Mankind;
(d) Coastal Zone Regimes; (e) Fisheries; (f) LLS & GDS; (g) Marine Scientific
Research; (h) International Dispute Settlement; (8) Shipping Law Certificates:
(a) Nationality, Registration and Ownership of Ships; (b) Proprietary Interests in
Ships; (c) Enforcement of Maritime Claims; (d) Carriage of Goods by Sea;
(e) Carriage of Passengers and their Luggage; (f) Maritime Labour Law; (g) Law
of Maritime Safety; (h) Law of Marine Collisions; (i) Law of Salvage and Wreck;
(j) Law of General Average; (k) Law of Towage; (l) Law of Marine Pilotage;
(m) Global Limitation of Liability; (n) Law of Marine Insurance
- George Washington University (www.gwu.edu). 1) International Security Policy
Certificate; (2) International Science and Technology Policy Certificate;
(3) International Trade Policy Certificate
- Southern New Hampshire University (www.snhu.edu). (1) Certificate in
International Business (online); (2) Certificate in International Finance (online)
- Thunderbird School of Global Management (www.thunderbird.edu).
(1) Executive Certificate in International Management (online); (2) Doing
Business in China Certificate (online)
- World Intellectual Property Organization (www.wipo.int). (1) Introduction to
the Patent Cooperation Treaty (online); (2) Trademarks, Industrial Designs and
Geographic Indications (online); (3) Arbitration and Mediation Procedure Under
the WIPO Rules (online)
- Hofstra University (http://www.hofstra.edu/Academics/grad/grad_postbacc.html).
International Business Certificate

Investigations
- Utica College (www.utica.edu). Financial Crimes Investigator Certificate
- Association of Certified Fraud Examiners (www.acfe.com). Certified Fraud
Examiner Designation
- Center for Legal Studies (www.legalstudies.com). Graduate Certificate in Legal
Investigation
- Southern New Hampshire University (www.snhu.edu). Certificate in Forensic
Accounting and Fraud Examination
- Association of Certified Anti-Money Laundering Specialists (www.acams.org).
Anti-Money Laundering Specialist Certificate

Investment Banking
- New York University (www.nyu.edu). Certificate in Investment Banking

Journalism

- University of Massachusetts (http://umass.edu). Online Certificate of Journalism

Labor & Employment

- eCornell (www.ecornell.com). Foundations of Employee Relations Certificate
- Rutgers University (www.rutgers.edu). Public Sector Labor Relations Certificate Program
- Mountain States Employers' Council (www.msec.org). (1) Employment Law Certificate Program; (2) Unions: Labor Relations Certificate Program; (3) Employee Handbooks: Revising or Developing; (4) Mediating Workplace Disputes; (5) Workplace Risk Management Certificate Program
- University of California-Davis Extension (http://extension.ucdavis.edu/certificates/). (1) Certificate in Labor-Management Relations; (2) Specialized Studies Program in Employee Relations
- Columbia Southern University (www.columbiasouthern.edu). Employment Law Specialist—Certification Program
- Expert Rating (www.expertrating.com). Employment Law Certification (online)
- CAI (www.capital.org). Employment Law Certification Series
- City University of New York (www.workered.org). The Murphy Institute—The Graduate Certificate in Labor Studies

Law and Business

- University of Pennsylvania (http://executiveeducation.wharton.upenn.edu). Wharton School—Wharton Business and Law Certificate
- Hofstra University (http://www.hofstra.edu/Academics/grad/grad_postbacc.html). International Business Certificate

Law Office Management

- Florida International University Legal Studies Institute (www.fiu.edu). Law Office Management Certificate
- Association of Legal Administrators (www.alanet.org). Certified Legal Manager Program

Legal Marketing

- University of Miami (www.educationmiami.edu). The UM Marketing Program for Lawyers

Legislation

- Georgetown University Government Affairs Institute (http://gai.georgetown.edu). Certificate Program in Legislative Studies

Licensing

- International Licensing Industry Merchandisers Association (www.licensing.org). Certificate in Licensing
- Licensing Executives Society (www.usa-canada.les.org). Intellectual Asset Management Certificates

- U.S. Department of Agriculture Graduate School (www.grad.usda.gov). Technology Transfer Program
- University of California, Berkeley Extension (www.unex.berkeley.edu). Certificate in Technology Transfer and Commercialization

Life Sciences
- American Health Lawyers Association (www.healthlawyers.org). Life Sciences Law Institute
- Indiana University Kelley School of Business (http://kelley.iu.edu). Kelley Executive Certificate in the Business of Life Sciences (ECBLS)
- University of Buffalo (www.buffalo.edu). Life Sciences Certificate Program

Local Government
- University of Missouri (www.umsl.edu/divisions/graduate/ppa/local-gov/certificate.html). St. Louis—Graduate Certificate Program in Local Government Management

Negotiation
- University of Notre Dame Mendoza School of Business (www.nd.edu). (1) Executive Certificate in Negotiation (online); (2) Advanced Negotiations Certificate (online)
- Center for International Humanitarian Cooperation (www.cihc.org). Humanitarian Negotiators Training Course

Nonprofit Management
- Capella University (www.capella.edu). Graduate Certificate in Management of Non-Profit Agencies
- American Society of Association Executives (www.asaecenter.org). Certified Association Executive
- Duke University (http://www.learnmore.duke.edu). Nonprofit Management Certificate
- Arizona State University (www.asu.edu). Graduate Certificate Program in Nonprofit Leadership and Management
- Northeastern University (www.spcs.neu.edu). Nonprofit Management Certificate (online option)

Privacy
- International Association of Privacy Professionals (www.iapp.org). (1) Certified Information Privacy Professional (CIPP); (2) Certified Information Privacy Professional/Government (CIPP/G)
- Institute of Consumer Financial Information (www.icfe.us). Certified Identity Theft Risk Management Specialist
- HIPAA Academy (www.trainforhipaa.com/certification.html). (1) Certified HIPAA Administrator; (2) Certified HIPAA Professional; (3) Certified HIPAA Security Specialist

- American Health Information Management Association (www.AHIMA.org). AHIMA Certified in Healthcare Privacy
- Joint Commission on Accreditation of Healthcare Organizations (www.jcaho.org). Privacy Certification Program for Business Associates
- HIPAA Training.Net (www.training-hipaa.net). (1) Certified HIPAA Privacy Expert; (2) Certified HIPAA Privacy Associate

Professional Liability
- American Board of Professional Liability Attorneys (www.abpla.org). (1) Medical Professional Liability Certificate; (2) Legal Professional Liability Certificate

Public Administration
- Central Michigan University (www.cmich.edu). Graduate Certificate in Public Administration
- Brookings Institution (www.brookings.edu/execed/certificateprograms.aspx). Certificate in Public Leadership

Public Policy
- North Carolina State University (http://pa.chass.ncsu.edu/prosStud/gradCert/publicPolicy.php). Public Policy Certificate Program
- University of Houston Hobby Center for Public Policy (www.uh.edu/hcpp/certification/cpm.htm). Certified Public Manager Program
- University of Southern California http://www.usc.edu/schools/sppd/programs/certificate/public_policy.html). Certificate in Public Policy
- City University of New York (www.workered.org). The Murphy Institute—Graduate Certificate in Public Administration and Public Policy
- American University (www.american.edu). Graduate Certificate in Public Policy Analysis

Real Estate
- University of Wisconsin (www.wisc.edu). Real Estate Certificate Program
- Chartered Realty Investor Society (www.crisociety.org). CRI Charter Designation: (1) Chartered Realty Investor One Certification; (2) Chartered Realty Investor Two Certification
- University of California-Davis Extension (http://extension.ucdavis.edu/certificates/). Certificate in Land Use and Environmental Planning
- International Right of Way Association—Right of Way Certification: (1) Asset (Property) Management; (2) Environmental Negotiation/Acquisition (www.irwaonline.org)

Regulatory Affairs
- Northeastern University (www.spcs.neu.edu). (1) Biopharmaceutical Domestic Regulatory Affairs; (2) Biopharmaceutical International Regulatory Affairs; (3) Medical Devices Regulatory Affairs
- San Diego State University (www.ces.sdsu.edu/regulatoryaffairs.html). Advanced Certificate in Regulatory Affairs

- Lehigh University (www.distance.lehigh.edu). Certificate in Regulatory Affairs in a Technical Environment

Securities
- Financial Industry Regulatory Agency (www.finra.com), (1) Compliance Boot Camp; (2) FINRA Institute at Wharton Certificate Program
- National Regulatory Services (www.nrs-inc.com). Investment Adviser Compliance Certificate Program

Tax
- University of San Diego School of Law (www.sandiego.edu). The Diploma in Taxation
- St. Thomas University (FL) School of Law (www.stu.edu/lawschool). Certificates in the International Tax Law Program: (1) International Financial Centers; (2) United States Taxation; (3) E-Commerce; (4) Anti-Money Laundering & Compliance; (5) Trusts and Estate Planning
- New York University School of Law (www.law.nyu.edu). Advanced Professional Certificate in Taxation
- Cleveland State University, Cleveland-Marshall School of Law (www.law.csuohio.edu). Tax Certificate Program
- Southern New Hampshire University (www.snhu.edu). Certificate in Taxation
- Bentley College (www.bentley.edu). Advanced Professional Certificate in Taxation
- National Business Institute (www.nbi-sems.com). Taxation Law Certificate

Technology Transfer
- U.S. Department of Agriculture Graduate School (www.grad.usda.gov). Technology Transfer Program
- University of California, Berkeley Extension (www.unex.berkeley.edu). Certificate in Technology Transfer and Commercialization
- University of Southern California—Marshall School of Business (www.marshall.usc.edu/tccm). Certificate in Technology Commercialization

Trial Advocacy
- National Board of Trial Advocacy (www.nbtanet.org). (1) Civil Trial Certificate (online); (2) Criminal Trial Certificate (online); (3) Family Law Certificate (online); (4) Social Security Disability Certificate (online)
- National College for DUI Defense (www.ncdd.com). DUI Defense Law Certificate

Training
- Texas A&M University (www.tamu.edu). Certified Training Professional
- International Import-Export Institute (http://expandglobal.com). Certified International Trade Educator

Victims' Rights
- Center for Legal Studies (www.legalstudies.com). Graduate Certificate in Victim Advocacy

Water Law

- United Nations Educational, Scientific and Cultural Organization (www.unesco.org). Water & Environmental Law and Institutions
- Oregon State University (http://ecampus.oregonstate.edu). Water Conflict Management Graduate Certificate (online)

Wealth Management

- University of California, Irvine (www.uci.edu). Personal Financial Planning Certificate
- New York Institute of Finance (www.nyif.com). Professional Certificate in Wealth Management

By Richard L. Hermann, Esq.

Excerpt, *From Lemons to Lemonade in the New Legal Job Market* (2012)

Getting the Most from Career & Outplacement Counseling

By Sheila Nielsen, JD

What are the two words you don't want to hear in the worst economy since the 1930s?

You're fired.

Lets face it, though: More than at any time in recent memory, that's been the reality for associates in practice groups without enough work, for associates and partners whose contract position is not being renewed, and for partners without portables. But all is not lost. After all, your firm's professional development person did say something about outplacement options. Which means you can choose to work with a career or outplacement counselor. But which counselor is best for you? What's more, how do you conduct a productive job search with a job market in deep freeze?

Here are eight points to consider:

Your counselor should help you discuss what you're going through.

Maybe outplacement sounds nicer than being fired or being let go, but it hurts just as much.

Most attorneys asked to leave their firms after working long hours and doing their best to succeed, feel a justifiable combination of betrayal, embarrassment, anger, and/or depression. In fact, some lawyers can become clinically depressed from job loss. To the point where it's hard to get up in the morning, and harder still to take the steps necessary to conduct a job search. In fact, some lawyers I've worked with feel such a sense of shame that they cannot tell anyone that they are looking for a new job. And others are so adrift they turn to alcohol or drugs.

A good counselor should encourage you to vent about whatever discomfort you are experiencing, including anger, frustration, sadness, self-doubt, and/or embarrassment. It helps to air your feelings, and to express yourself outside of the confines of the law firm. If your counselor is a trained therapist, all the better; if not, your counselor must at least be capable of identifying a clinical depression and help you to get medical attention for that condition if it does occur.

Your counselor should help you improve your game.

One of the most important things you want to learn from outplacement is why you might have been let go in the first place, and how to avoid the same fate later. Your counselor should help you find out why your workplace targeted you, what made you vulnerable, and to help you recognize and overcome whatever problem(s) might have led to your loss of this job. An employer will rarely if ever tell you this directly.

I have worked with associates who, fairly or not, did not have the partner's trust to work at their class level. As a result, the associate was passed over, and the partner(s) used associates they believed to be more capable. Perhaps the associate made too many mistakes, perhaps they expressed uncertainty about their ability to handle matters, perhaps they were slow to turn the work around, perhaps they performed with too many errors. Or, perhaps the associate asked a few too many questions, leading the partners to use another associate who performed more efficiently.

A good counselor is able to read between the lines when given somewhat coded information about the outplaced associate or partner. A good counselor will work with that lawyer to improve his or her game as well as to demystify the often-opaque reviews that sound reasonably good but actually reflect an individual's shortcomings.

The kiss of death for many partners is their lack of business origination. I have worked with many partners who were let go because they did not know nor want to know how to develop business. Unfortunately, many of today's more senior partners entered the workplace before business development became a requirement for job security. They never learned how to build a practice, and some would like to avoid business development in the future as well. But, depending on one's practice area, client development has become a necessity.

A good outplacement experience includes coaching to learn more productive ways to deal with workplace situations that are problematic for you, and ways to manage or cope with such problems as procrastination or organization and time management. If you get nothing else out of your outplacement experience, this knowledge about how to change your game for the better is worth its weight in gold.

Your counselor should help you assess whether to leave the law and how to make that transition.

Another question that may need addressing is whether law is even the right game for you.

After being let go, it's only natural you would wonder if your choice of a legal career was a mistake. After all, practicing law does not meet everyone's needs. Some lawyers who are outplaced say they have not been enjoying their jobs, and maybe it showed. I have worked with disappointed lawyers who tell me their dream had always been to do something to make the world a better place. But in most law firms lawyers rarely have a mission that satisfies that wish, and pro bono work is hard to manage when you are an overworked associate or partner.

Doubts about a career in the law also arise from other common sources of dissatisfaction: long hours, billable hours, lack of a work/life balance, difficult partners, demanding clients, lack of interest in the law itself, and the workplace culture itself. Many of these stressful concerns will prompt soul-searching about whether to continue as a lawyer. Outplacement is an opportunity to look at other prospects for a future career and identify a more meaningful direction.

Not all counselors know how to assess the issue of career change effectively.

Done well, self-assessment work is a mixture of vocational counseling and insight-oriented work. And yes, it can at times even border on therapy! Your counselor should be able to guide you through a process that includes a work history and personal history, as well as a series of exercises that allow you to think outside the box about work that would be a better fit. If you are considering a new career direction, you will benefit from a counselor who has worked with many lawyers and helped many of them to launch new careers or change their practice area or move into a different sector of the field of law such as government, not-for-profit, or trade associations.

> Recently, I worked with a conflict-avoidant litigator. He's bright, soft-spoken, studious, thoughtful and shied away from confrontation most of his life. It was as though conflict avoidance was hardwired into his DNA. And this failure to confront, argue, and aggressively litigate was seen as a serious weakness, of course, and he was eventually outplaced by his firm. Recruiters tried to interest him in similar positions, which is only natural for a recruiter to do since they earn their fee by finding jobs that fit the current skill set of a candidate. Fortunately, this lawyer took the time to do some self-assessment and wisely decided against pursuing another litigation position. Had he accepted one, it's likely he would have failed again.

People cannot radically change a major personality trait. No amount of exhorting, even by Dr. Phil, will do the trick. Far better to help a lawyer move to a job where he can be a stand-out for being himself.

A good outplacement coach ought to help an attorney with a case of severe career mismatch to identify likely places in the field of law where doing an excellent job does not require a personality lobotomy, and where the move is realistically possible to accomplish. This particular client left litigation for a government job where his strengths in investigation, research, and writing are all called into play. He enjoys his work, and is likely to be very successful.

Your counselor should be psychologically astute & realistic.

Some vocational counselors will stop their work with a prospective career changer at the point when that person has identified a career direction that seems to be a better fit. But there is still more work to be done. The new career direction has to be something that is doable and realistic given the person's situation. Would this career change necessitate re-credentialing? If so, can and will the person do that? What is his or her financial situation and home situation? Is the person motivated enough to make this change? These are just a few of the questions that the counselor should be assessing.

Many people say they want to change their careers but are ambivalent to the point of being incapable of making the change they desire. The psychology of ambivalence is complex.

For example, some people dream about a new career but won't take steps to further their dream. In fact the dream itself sustains them, and if it is challenged, or removed, the person may become depressed. Motivation to change can also be dampened by a fear of failure or lack of self-esteem. A good counselor should be able to recognize these and similar psychological issues, and help the lawyer work through his or her roadblock, develop a longer-term plan for career change, accept that s/he is wedded to the status quo, or help them to add satisfaction through activities outside of work.

And even if the career-changer is motivated enough and can launch a viable effort to make a career direction change, most people need some form of continued coaching or guidance to leave the law and successfully transition into the new field. Without that support, many lawyers end up falling back into a job that might be undesirable for them but will pay the bills. Their doubts about the law often linger, and undermine long-term career satisfaction.

Many lawyers who take the time to assess the rightness of their legal career discover that, in fact, the law is a good vocation after all. That the grass is not always greener.

If you are unhappy at work, it might seem as if you need to get out of the law. But your dissatisfaction might vanish if you are able to work with a more compatible group of people, or lose the boss-from-hell, or work fewer hours. Some lawyers who take the time to assess their career direction will decide to stay in the law, but the difference is that they know more about what they need from the next legal job, and they make a thought-out choice to stay. Not all legal workplaces are alike, and it is unfair to paint them with too broad a brush. An outplacement counselor should understand the legal work world as distinct from the business work world in order to guide a lawyer to a better-fitting job in the law.

Your counselor should know how to coach your job interview.

Doubts about being a lawyer are important to address if for no other reason than this: a good interview cannot be faked.

People are too good at reading credibility for you to try to pretend you are thrilled at the prospect of working at a particular place when you really couldn't care less. If you are not interested, your demeanor and body language subtly convey that disinterest, which has a negative impact on the interviewer. Even ambivalence can usually be detected by an astute interviewer unless you are a really good actor or actress.

Your counselor can help you to perfect your interview approach by doing a mock interview and asking you all the questions that usually get asked in a standard interview as well as any you are afraid a potential employer might decide to ask you. Your counselor should be able to help you answer all questions honestly, and with the strongest response possible as well as provide feedback on your demeanor and dress.

You should also be helped to craft a strong statement of advocacy punctuated by anecdotal evidence that supports your contention that you would be a good match for this job and why. The counselor should provide a framework for interviewing, and that framework should be shaped to the job for which you are interviewing.

Your counselor should understand the legal market.

It is possible that a different practice area, or a switch to government or another sector of the field of law, might satisfy more of your workplace needs, be a better match for your personality, and maximize your chances to land a job even in the current market. If so, you will need to understand how to make that switch.

The success of such an attempted move may hinge on whether you can convince the next employer that it is a good idea to hire you even if your skill set is not a perfect match.

What should you say to advocate for yourself?

What should you say or not say about why you want to make this move?

A good outplacement coach should be able to help you, and not simply insist that you stay in the same practice area.

Of course your coach also needs to help you to assess whether this career move is realistic given all the variables: the ability to transfer your skills, how well you can make the case for yourself, the economic climate, etc. You may need to shift your career in stages, developing a new direction by attending conferences, joining committees, doing pro bono work in your area of interest, or returning to school to improve your credentials for a new career direction. Part of self-assessment is about market need.

For example, think of the job market in terms of appetite.

When a particular market expands, it is very hungry and needy, and a transition into that market is easier. During the dot-com era, lawyers without perfect credentials moved into that rapidly expanding field in a fairly wide variety of roles from in-house to business side to IT. At the moment, we have a legal job market many of whose practice areas have little or no appetite. Which means that career transitions will be limited and employers will be very picky. There may still be need, however, in bankruptcy, benefits, IP, and litigation, and markets in Asia may still be hungry for lawyers in certain practice areas that reflect continued growth rather than contraction.

But because we are in the shadow of a recession, a radical career transition that might have been possible before may have to be worked on for a longer time, and even landing a job in the same practice area could be a challenge requiring job search strategies that might not have been so crucial to success before this meltdown began. And by search strategies, I mean strategies that go beyond mailed resumes, answering ads, and the usual networking tropes.

In the current economic climate, companies and law firms will be less likely to use recruiters if and when they have a need. To be successful in this extraordinary market, a job seeker must use more advanced techniques and strategies for networking and will usually need more close coaching from the outplacement counselor as well.

Not every counselor understands how to teach attorneys more sophisticated networking search techniques. I base that comment on the numbers of lawyers I work with who report their prior or even current outplacement experiences to me, and say that they do not have a grasp of the kinds of more advanced networking strategies I am alluding to. As part of a more sophisticated networking search, for example, you need to tell a consistent story to the potential employer by utilizing informal interviews which are supported by your résumé or bio.

Your counselor should know how to help you tell your story.

Your résumé is your particular way of telling your story. There are few hard and fast rules about how to construct your résumé, and it can be challenging for the job seeker to craft a résumé that he or she feels confident about.

A resume needs to be crafted based on the particular job one is interviewing for, which means that the résumé will usually highlight particular parts of your background depending on the position you seek. A résumé might also have a different look depending on whether the job seeker is trying to land the same kind of job or is trying to move into a different field or practice area. Close attention needs to be paid to the transferable skills that a potential employer will need to see in order to give the job seeker a shot at an interview. The résumé must be just right when it has the potential to get you into the pool of applicants that will be vetted for the job. A standard business-style résumé is not always the best approach for a lawyer, and sometimes outplacement groups do not seem to know that. Your counselor should know that some law firms are more comfortable with a very readable chronological resume with an attached deal sheet, for example, and help you to craft that version of your background if you are shooting for that market rather than in-house.

Your counselor should suggest knowledgeable legal recruiters when appropriate.

If you create a relationship with a recruiter, it is important to tell him or her about any other search efforts you are engaged in so that they are not stepping on anyone's toes. Good recruiters have to guard their good reputations because their livelihoods depend on the trust of their employers, namely, law firms and corporations. So you need to be honest with your recruiter. If you were let go because you were dealing drugs in the office lunchroom, don't say you were let go because your group was slow. On the other hand, if you need to move on because you blew a crucial deadline, and the sole partner you work with went ballistic and vowed never to give you work again in this lifetime, but your background is stellar in every other way, you should tell your recruiter about this aberration and see what she or he says about it.

SHEILA NIELSEN, JD, IS A CHICAGO-BASED LAW CAREER COUNSELOR

Homework Assignments

Assignment #1: Most Satisfying Work Experience

Think of three work experiences that gave you satisfaction. These should be specific actual events, rather than a general statement of what you like. Write a short summary of each experience. You can draw on experiences as a lawyer as well as from summer or part-time jobs, non-law jobs, volunteer or charitable work, or any other work experience you've had since age 18.

Assignment #2: What Success Means to Me

Write a short essay called, *"What Success Means to Me"*. Make it personal and succinct. The idea is to identify, in a personal way, what is important to you in a work experience.

Assignment #3: People Whose Jobs I Admire

List six people whose jobs you admire. Write down their name and a brief description of what they do (full sentences, not phrases). Then add three or four additional sentences that explains what appeals to you about their job. These can be people that you know personally or who are public figures living or dead.

Assignment #4: Pictures Speak a Thousand Words

Go through picture magazines, and cut out any photos that capture some quality that you want to be experiencing in your job. Paste each one on a separate piece of paper, and write down a sentence or two for each one, describing what the photo represents. The pictures can be literal (e.g., a photo of someone advising a client), or symbolic (e.g., a photo of a bird in flight, symbolizing "freedom"), or a combination of both. Note: Be sure you don't omit the second part of this assignment, writing a sentence that describes what the photo represents—this is the part of the exercise that will yield the most insights.

Assignment #5: My Obituary

Assume that you have found some career that finally suits you, and you lived the remainder of your life the way you wish. Write your obituary in the third person, and be sure to include some information about how this person (i.e., you!) will be remembered, what s/he contributed, what s/he did for a living, and whatever else would capture the essence of what you were known for. I realize that this will require speculation on your part, and you may have no certainty about what you write, but do your best.

Assignment #6: Interviews

Talk to five individuals (friends, colleagues) who know you really well. Interview them about your career direction, and write down verbatim what they tell you. This part is very important! Typical questions that you might ask them include "Since you've known me, have I ever expressed a burning desire to do a particular occupation?" Or, "Knowing me as you do, is there a particular job that you see me doing?"

Assignment #7: Self-Assessment

- Finish these sentences in some detail:
  I don't like to admit it, but I really need…
  I feel happiest when I'm…
  If money and education were not considerations, the kind of work I prefer would be…
  When I was a child, I always wanted to be a…
  Time passes most quickly for me when I'm…
- Imagine you've won a $200,000 lottery annuity. Describe how it would change your daily existence.
- For one week, take a few minutes every day to jot a few key thoughts about your ideal workplace. Describe your ideal workplace in detail. If others are there, who are they and what are they doing?
- For a full month, make note of which daily activities you enjoyed the most and the least. At the end of the month, summarize and categorize your preferences.
- For a full month, take a few minutes every day to visualize your ideal day. Describe it even if it has nothing to do with work.
- In 10 minutes of continuous writing (without removing your pen from the paper or your fingers from the keyboard), describe what you enjoy doing when you're not working.
- Write a description of yourself. Describe your interests and define your personal style, including the way you like to dress, live, and interact with others.

- Describe what you know of your long-range career goals, and identify what contributions you would like to make to yourself, to your family, to your community, and to the world.
- At the end of the exercise, look for themes and contradictions. Summarize the results in writing.

Assignment #8: Passions

Describe up to three dozen of the most enjoyable events of your life. Focus on experiences you remember as fun or fulfilling, and when time seem to pass without notice. Choose events you enjoyed as they were unfolding, not because of any outcome or positive feedback. Be sure to include at least a dozen experiences from childhood:

- How often were you alone and how often with others? What were you doing when you were alone? How did those activities differ from your activities with others?
- How many others were with you? What was the nature of your interaction with them? Were you conversing or participating with them, or quietly working alongside them? Were you engaged in group activity? What kind?
- What were the characteristics of the people around you? Upbeat? Analytical? Daring? Supportive? Competitive? Challenging? Smart? Artistic? Athletic?
- What were you doing? Was it physical, mental or both? Were you passive or active, moving around or staying in one place; conveying or receiving information?
- What was the purpose of your participation in each event? Personal growth, building something, enjoyment, making change, helping others, competition?
- In what environments did you find yourself? Indoors or outside, sunny, rainy, dark, bright, crowded, spacious, formal, informal?
- Were you relating emotionally, intellectually, physically or spiritually to your surroundings?
- Were your activities internalized—that is, thoughtful or meditative or external to yourself—for example, teaching, advising, coaching, viewing entertainment?

Assignment #9: Your Fantasy Employment

Imagine yourself working at a fantasy job, and describe a day-in-the-life in this role. Be as specific and detailed as you like, and imagine yourself in this role from your first cup of coffee to the end of the day.

Where are you?

What are your surroundings?

What activities are underway around you?

Who, if anyone, are you working with?

What are the others doing, and what are you doing in relation to them?

If no one else is around, what are you doing?

Assignment #10: The Real Costs of Change

This assignment asks that you project yourself through time—1, 5, 10, even 20 years—and describe what your life might look like if you remained on your present course. Describe your life in terms of opportunities, relationships, and your emotional and physical well-being.

The Values Card Sort Model

The Values Card Sort is a simple and effective way to identify the values that you most and least want in a job.

THE INSTRUCTIONS, PART I

1. Cut pages 209 through 219 from the book and separate the cards. You should have a deck of 5 **Category Cards** (*Always Valued, Often Valued,* etc.) and 48 **Value Cards**, each of which contains a value you might find attractive in the workplace.

2. Place the five Category Cards side by side. Then sort and assign all 48 Value Cards to the appropriate columns, placing those you would value most highly in an ideal job under the "Always Valued" column, and those values about which you care less strongly in the other appropriate columns. *Don't spend too much time analyzing the exercise; it works best if you sort as quickly as possible.*

3. Now, rearrange the cards within each column so they are ranked in priority order. In other words, your very strongest value will be at the top of "Always Valued," and the least attractive value will be at the bottom of "Never Valued." Resist the temptation to arrange and rearrange several times; your first instinct is usually your truest. NOTE: You cannot have more than eight cards in the "Always Valued" column (only when you are forced to choose between competing desirable values do your "true" top values rise to the surface).

4. When you are finished sorting, write down the values you selected in the exact order that your cards are laid out in each column.

Always Valued	Often Valued	Sometimes Valued	Seldom Valued	Never Valued
_____	_____	_____	_____	_____
_____	_____	_____	_____	_____
_____	_____	_____	_____	_____
_____	_____	_____	_____	_____
_____	_____	_____	_____	_____
_____	_____	_____	_____	_____
_____	_____	_____	_____	_____
_____	_____	_____	_____	_____

5. In two weeks, repeat this exercise…but without looking at the earlier results. It is very important that your second card sort be independent of the first. As before, write down the values in the exact order that your cards are laid out in each column.

Always Valued	Often Valued	Sometimes Valued	Seldom Valued	Never Valued
_____	_____	_____	_____	_____
_____	_____	_____	_____	_____
_____	_____	_____	_____	_____
_____	_____	_____	_____	_____
_____	_____	_____	_____	_____
_____	_____	_____	_____	_____
_____	_____	_____	_____	_____
_____	_____	_____	_____	_____

6. A minimum of two rounds of card sorting are necessary for this exercise; a third is optional. If you do a third sort, wait another two weeks before completing the exercise so you won't be influenced by the results of your previous card sort.

THE INSTRUCTIONS, PART II

After the second sorting (two weeks apart), please return to Page 44 for the remaining four exercises. In this way, you will have completely identified the values that you most and least want in a job.